SEEING IS DECEIVING
Detecting in the Dark

Front cover: Acajou ever vigilant
Back cover: The author with her guide dog

Seeing is Deceiving:
Detecting in the Dark

by

A D Whittenbury

Illustrations by Louise Hodgkinson

ELSP

Published in 2013
and reprinted 2013 by
ELSP
11 Regents Place
Bradford on Avon
Wiltshire   BA15 1ED

Origination by Ex Libris Press
www.ex-librisbooks.co.uk

Printed in Britain by
Orbit Digital Print
Cortsham, Wiltshire

Typeset in 11/14 point Century Schoolbook

ISBN 978-1-906641-54-2

© 2013 A D Whittenbury

© 2013 Louise Hodgkinson

Contents

Chapter 1	Where was He?	7
Chapter 2	Notices	20
Chapter 3	Pins and Needles	31
Chapter 4	Rather Fishy	44
Chapter 5	No Mouse? The Technical Approach	54
Chapter 6	Cat Tales	59
Chapter 7	The Mystery Caller	63
Chapter 8	Troublesome Neighbours	75
Chapter 9	Reversed Charges	81
Chapter 10	Picnic at Dawn	92
Chapter 11	Introducing Terry and Nige	105
Chapter 12	Forsaken	111
Chapter 13	The Feathered Refugees	113
Chapter 14	A Chill Wind	127
Chapter 15	Idiosyncrasies	146

Chapter 1

Where was He?

Having scored a faint star with the point of a sharp knife on the flattened dome, she slipped her fingers beneath the rim to grasp the flimsy frill and retract neat petals of silky skin. Preoccupied by mushroom peeling in preparation for a mixed grill, it was not until Leonie heard the time signal for the seven o'clock news that she remembered to make the routine cat check.

For some reason, Toga, her guide dog, seemed restive this evening. It was unseasonably warm for Thursday, the 20th of October and as the temperature did not equate with darkness in her mind, she had neglected to close the cat flap – a necessary precaution at night for the safety of the three Burmese feline members of the household. When winter approached and the days grew noticeably shorter, Leonie used to consult her Braille copy of the *Radio Times* to discover the exact moments of sunrise and sunset so that as darkness fell she could switch on the lights to make the house look inhabited and welcoming when her husband, Andrew, came home.

The two females, Suchard (pronounced Sooshar) and Paprika, one a Chocolate Burmese cat and the other a Red, were entwined in a sleeping embrace on an armchair in the sitting room but Acajou (pronounced Aca shoo like a sneeze), Suchard's handsome dark brown son, was nowhere to be found. She was not too perturbed at first, however, as she had only done a hasty finger-tip investigation of beds, chairs, the laundry basket and the woolly mat on top of the boiler. Andrew would be home soon and he could conduct a thorough visual search. When he eventually arrived more than an hour later, his hunt proved to be no more effective. Secretly, Leonie began to panic and while he ate his somewhat dehydrated dinner, she put the harness and lead on Toga and together they set out to visit some of Acajou's favourite haunts.

Leonie crossed Lingham Way to the corner house on the opposite side of their quiet cul-de-sac where there was a low wall, softened in spring time by pale mauve aubrietia and sheltered throughout the year by the waxy leaves of a mature camellia. This was a highly favoured vantage point from which the Burmese contingent liked to watch the comings and goings of all things that moved in Lingham Way. She called and meowed, *sotto voce*, lest she should be thought somewhat strange by neighbours, but there was no response. Continuing round the corner, Leonie

Where was He?

then crossed the spasmodically busy Pine Hill Avenue to a narrow lane that led, after about three hundred yards, to the wrought iron gates of Lingham Park. For the first hundred yards or so, the path was flanked on either side by an untamed verge with bushes, trees and brambles and, towards the end of summer, flowers grew in profusion with grasses so tall that trailing fingers would set to flight a cloud of feathery seeds. Hemlock, convolvulus and vetches abounded and more painful to note, thistles and nettles flourished providing a haven for both the hunter and the hunted.

The building on the right of the entrance to the lane housed a gymnasium and cricket school and there were times when the traffic on Pine Hill Avenue was reminiscent of the dodgems at a funfair. The young hopefuls along with the ageing perennials were just leaving the cricket school as Leonie and Toga crossed the road into the lane. In the last year, two tennis courts had been built towards the far end of the lane where previously there had been a field with horses. The whole area provided an excellent setting for hunting sprees. If she gave Toga a free run there, Acajou would come towards her calling, sounding almost forlorn with his plaintive voice which always finished on a downward inflection in a minor key but, on this occasion – not a sound!

Andrew, who had by now finished his meal, came to meet her and together, they walked to the park gate but it was very dark and he could see virtually nothing. By this time, all the cricketers had gone home and there was no one to ask about the possible sighting of a dark brown Burmese cat so they walked on down Pine Hill Avenue to the school gates. The school drive was shielded from the gardens behind the houses in Lingham Way by trees and a beech hedge where once they had seen a dead fox in the ditch but the gates were closed and they had to postpone the search until the morning when the school caretaker would come to unlock them.

Leonie confined the two girl cats to the main part of the house by closing the internal kitchen door so that the cat flap could be left open throughout the night lest Acajou should return of his own accord. He might have been delayed, merely confused, having been lured into strange territory by his incorrigible curiosity but Leonie was gradually becoming convinced that he had been detained against his will.

As the outside wall was very thick, Andrew had fixed a conventional cat flap externally to replace the air vent grill and had lined the tunnel through the wall with coconut matting so that paws could be cleansed on entry thus avoiding numerous muddy footprints on the quarry tiles in the kitchen. Internally, he had devised another little door that could be slid open and hooked up with a string loop. Both flaps were perforated to maintain the circulation of fresh air.

At eleven o'clock Andrew retired to bed but Leonie went out into the garden once more and then into the road to call again and to listen but without success.

She locked the back door and said goodnight to Toga, who was already asleep in her basket, before going upstairs only to find that Suchard and Paprika had also retired for the night and were safely shut in the bathroom; their nocturnal freedom having to be curtailed in order to ensure a modicum of peace in the house.

She was restless. Was Acajou lying injured at the roadside or possibly locked in the changing room at the cricket school? Perhaps he had strayed into a garage, bent on rodent catching and was trapped – waiting – erroneously secure in the knowledge that every day ended with a good meal, a hug and a snug bed curled between Suchard and Paprika.

She found it difficult to sleep and went downstairs several times during the night to see if the kitchen door had been moved. Having left it only just ajar, any change would have been obvious. There was none. She crept back upstairs to bed and tried to lie very still and concentrate on "positive thinking". As she wrestled to clear the screen of her hyperactive imagination, the picture of a ring doughnut seemed to appear and dimly remembered words filtered through her semi-consciousness:

'Twixt optimist and pessimist
The difference is droll;
The optimist sees the doughnut,
The pessimist, the hole.

At six a.m. Leonie decided to get up and to search again.

If Acajou had been harmed in a feral skirmish, he still might have strength enough to call out to Toga should he hear her. There was no time to be lost! She took some clothes from the chair beside the bed and tiptoed out of the bedroom leaving Andrew to sleep until aroused by the alarm. His days were long and arduous at hospital and she knew that for him a full night's sleep was essential. She dressed downstairs, slipped the harness over Toga's head, clipped the lead onto her collar and together, they resumed their quest. The birds had not yet started to sing so she realised it must still be dark. The moments of crystal silence before dawn were perfect for the listener and she was less fearful in the morning darkness than in the shadows of the night. Although Leonie was unable to see light at all, her imagination was active. This time, they walked up the hill towards the main road to see if they could find Acajou in one of the gardens alongside it but there was no sign of him; no rustling, no mewing.

    Andrew was up and showered by the time she returned and he said he would come with her as soon as it was light. Suchard and Paprika trotted downstairs when the bathroom door was opened but, without pausing for a drink or checking their food bowls, they hurried through their little cat tunnel into the garden as though off to search for the absentee; they knew something was amiss. Paprika ran straight out under the gate and across the road, muttering purposefully, and vanished into the gardens opposite to reappear a few minutes later and take up her position on the low wall at the corner but only briefly. She was accustomed to being accompanied by Acajou or Suchard and the latter was busy inspecting every nook and cranny in her own garden.

    Having no luck down by the park gate, Andrew and Leonie turned their attention to the area around the tennis courts and then beyond the pavilion to the paddock where Toga was able to run free. Leonie removed the harness, unfastened the lead from the collar and gave the end of it to Andrew so as to maintain contact with him but with a loose link which gave her a little more freedom while guidance was still readily available. She loved him to hold her hand as it made her feel secure and confident, especially in difficult or crowded settings, but she was happy to walk freely in wide open spaces. Together, they scoured the boundaries, and particularly the side which was bordered by woodland and the park where Acajou was wont to explore. When Leonie tried mimicking some feline sounds, a gull took off from a goal post shrieking with indignation and, high in the branches of an elm, rooks cawed their disapproval at the sudden disturbance. To the hypersensitive ear, one or

Where was He?

two of the less raucous cries resembled those of an animal in distress. Alas! There was no trace of Acajou so, once again, the lead was clipped to Toga's collar and, somewhat dejectedly, they left the paddock to check on the cricket school and the gymnasium. There, too, they drew a blank.

One is not expected to be seen creeping around neighbours' gardens and peering behind dustbins at 7.30 a.m. so it was with diffidence that they searched the length of Lingham Way. In a small market town like Castleridge, there were those by whom circumspect behaviour and boring conventionality were deemed to be of utmost importance.

Leonie recalled, with a little guilt, that only the previous week, she had made just such a judgement when a patient coyly confided that her hobby was keeping "fancy wats".

The first session in the clinic is taken up by the assessment of the patient's condition when the physiotherapist asks numerous questions including the nature of work and hobbies and there is little time for appraisal of personality, but Mrs Hardwick's excitable manner, her nervous laugh and a slight speech defect had alerted Leonie's interest.

Subsequently, sitting with her foot immersed in a plastic bath of warm water, muscles twitching rhythmically, stimulated by the rise and fall of a Faradic current, the patient began to talk more freely. The flat shoes and tweedy jacket and conversation peppered with down-to-earth remarks did not immediately suggest a colourful personality. It is surprising how much can be picked up by a blind physiotherapist from examining feet, inspecting footwear and checking posture. Mrs Hardwick found the foot exercises, rolling a tennis ball under each foot and picking up marbles with her toes entertaining but found the balancing exercises rather difficult and needed to put her hand on the plinth for support when trying to stand on the Wobble Board; a piece of wood approximately 50 centimetres square with a hemispherical base. Leonie had then discussed weight with Mrs Hardwick wondering if this could be relevant to her foot problem and, if so, advise her that she could possibly begin to tackle this problem by looking out for any "eating triggers" and attempt to avoid perhaps further weight increase. Mrs Hardwick neighed self-consciously and confessed that one such had been the cause of her downfall. Living in London, she said, until 1984, friends frequently called to see her but, since she had moved to this town, she had become lonely and, seeing an article in *The Times* about fancy rats, she had been fascinated.

"After work each day," she explained, "I go to the shops to buy fwesh gweens and a packet of salad if it is being sold off cheaply in the evening."

Leonie lavished praise on her for her commendable effort but she interrupted,

"Oh no, no. You don't understand. The gweens are not for me; they are for my pet wats and when I have finished at the salad counter, I tend to wander over to the home-baked cakes and I'm afraid I just can't wesist a bargain. They have cheap offers there too."

On further probing she was keen to elaborate and it became apparent that she owned five rats who lived in two spacious cages in the second bedroom. Mr Hardwick seemed to have disappeared.

"I have two vawieties," she continued, "Hercules, Zeus and Flossy who are bwown wats. They live in one cage and Adam and Eve live in the other and are white. Each one knows his or her own name," she insisted. By the time Mrs Hardwick had dried her feet, learned her exercises, dressed and left the cubicle, Leonie was able to readjust her mental picture and to record notes with a host of

Where was He?

intriguing details.

Her thoughts returned to the present as she and Toga made their way back home and Andrew glanced into all the parked cars and tapped on their boots. There was just a chance that Acajou might be shut inside one of these as he had a penchant for vehicles of any breed. The Mercedes next door, a removal van or a milk float were all of equal interest to him. On a sunny day, he would relax on the bonnet of their family car. A large copper beech overhung the drive and Acajou could watch the pigeons grooming themselves on the high branches. Although they were no further forward in tracing Acajou, some solace could be derived from the fact that no body had been found or signs of any animal warfare.

Approximately once a month, Leonie's sister, who lived near London Bridge, came over to spend the morning with her and she arrived, brisk and bright, at half past eight; a good time to travel as, minutes later, the school traffic tends to clog up the system. She was always eager to help with anything and to search for a missing cat was a good way for her to start the day and to diffuse her abundant energy. Elizabeth was a little taller than Leonie, enviably slim and invariably smartly dressed. Leonie smiled as her sister clipped along the pavements beside her in her high heels feeling like a country cousin in her navy blue anorak and dog walking shoes bought especially for the purpose. Her sister had never owned a pair of Wellingtons, let alone green ones.

Elizabeth had looked after a dog for seven years, a silver-grey Lhasa Apso, inherited when their parents died but he was more of an ornamental pet; a lapsed show dog who fell from his prize winner's pedestal at the age of nine months or so when his full complement of teeth failed to materialise. His long, silky hair was difficult to manage

15

and, when it completely obscured his eyes, a design feature to protect him from snow-blindness – not a serious threat in Surrey – he had to suffer the indignity of a visit to the Poodle Parlour for a severe trim. Silver's exercise used to consist of pavement excursions in suburbia or jollity in the garden pursuing badger scents after which his feet would be meticulously dried and his coat thoroughly brushed.

Toga, Leonie was ashamed to confess, was less frequently groomed but a mixed climate made it necessary for her, too, to tolerate a good deal of paw care. Prevention of muddy foot marks was simpler for Leonie than their removal. In fact, even the cats had to suffer, when coming in from the rain and if Leonie was quick enough to catch them, a brief rub down with a navy blue frog-bedecked flannel, a diminutive version of Toga's towel. Toga's shiny black coat required little attention and, as she was a slim dog, she had a sleek and generally healthy appearance. Her warm, brown eyes and gentle face evoked both admiration and affection from kindly members of the public who never failed to be astonished by the effervescence they concealed. When Leonie and Toga were out shopping in the High Street, visiting the bakery, for example, the mouth-watering smells tended to cause lapses in her concentration and even though a fully trained guide dog, Leonie had trouble in exerting her authority. Queuing was a tricky technique to master. They had to rely on prods and nudges to achieve synchronous progression with the herd and, if Toga sat or lay down when they were stationary as recommended by the rule book, a stray foot soon trod on a tail tip or toe and she would leap up surprising the person in the line ahead, sometimes with a cursory but ticklish sniff. Also, when you are a long dog in a crowded shop, it is not easy to stand without your chin overhanging a shopping basket or your nose being buried in the back of an unsuspecting

Where was He?

knee. Leonie could only guess what was going on when she heard uncertain laughter or …

"Good heavens! I wondered who was doing that!"

Alternatively, "Ooh-ah, I think it is my sausages she's after."

Now and then, a friendly soul would whisper an explanation. Exuberant tail wagging was a sure sign of a smile or a friendly scratch behind the ear but, once or twice, she surpassed herself by shocking or delighting a nose-high toffee-sucking toddler with a kiss.

Toga had many winning ways but instant obedience was not one of them. Her response to a summons was rarely immediate and if the distraction was more interesting than her owner, she manifested supreme indifference. About five months after Toga qualified, this caused a near disaster. Having spent the afternoon in a wildfowl reserve, where her behaviour was impeccable, Leonie and Andrew took her to Rustington beach which was completely deserted, probably due to buffeting winds. Leonie removed her harness and unclipped the lead. Toga shook herself thoroughly, looked up at a couple of seagulls and circled around them twice before suddenly shooting off at a tangent straight into the sea following the seagulls who were struggling against the gale. Frantically, Andrew and Leonie called but to no avail as the wild wind hurled their alternate pleas and rebukes back to them. Andrew ran to the water's edge but Toga would not have been able to hear with the wind and the waves lapping around her ears as she swam, apparently on her way to France. Indulging in her addiction to water, her blissful swim continued for several minutes. Fortunately, however, her progress was impeded by a natural curve in the shoreline and, still following one of the seagulls, her feet once again were on *terra* moderately *firma*. Andrew took Leonie by

17

the hand to guide her, helping her to avoid the pools and larger pebbles and together they set off, as speedily as the wind would permit, along the beach but by the time they reached Toga, she had collapsed, panting, on to the soggy wet sand. Postponing the deserved admonishment, Leonie attached the lead to secure their prize. This episode was a salutary warning for Toga's breathless guardians.

    Elizabeth and Leonie repeated the search in the more promising localities as by nine o'clock the sun was shining and Leonie hoped that the warmth and brightness might withdraw Acajou from his place of night refuge. They decided not to cross the busy road at the top of the hill to hunt in the Memorial Gardens even though there was a pond with goldfish, an enticing prospect for any self-respecting cat. Across the little wooden bridge there was a large lawn surrounded by well-tended flower beds and then a bandstand where the children used to play when they were small, running around and enjoying the stage, shouting to hear the echoes. Beyond the bandstand, where a brass band sometimes played on a Sunday afternoon in the summer, there was a cricket ground said to be the oldest in the country. Leonie knew this area well as she and Andrew used to linger by the raised herb bed so that she could touch and crush the leaf of the most fragrant herbs and check the leaf formation or scent of any new plants to be added to her collection in the herb tubs in their garden. Then, she would sometimes buy one when they next visited the Garden Centre for a pot of Earl Grey tea and a spoily piece of cake on a Sunday afternoon.

    However, as there was no untamed area with prolific vegetation to afford Acajou shelter, Elizabeth and Leonie decided to return home. If he had left the district as an unwilling or unwitting passenger in a vehicle, it would be impossible to guess where he had finished his journey.

Where was He?

The sunshine had brought some of the neighbours out into their gardens, two of whom generously offered to ask other residents of Lingham Way to check their garages and their sheds. It transpired that school half-term had started and four of the families had already gone away on holiday and Leonie feared the worst. If Acajou was imprisoned, he would have to wait many days before being released.

After a cup of coffee and an exchange of family news, it was time for Elizabeth to leave. They both made all kinds of sensible remarks about the clement weather and agreed that cats were prone to short spells of absence returning usually after one or two days, none the worse for the experience.

Chapter 2

Notices

Leonie decided to write a host of notices for widespread distribution. As she could not search thoroughly for him herself, the notion that several pairs of eyes were doing so on her behalf did console her. She had a computer with a speech synthesiser which, when activated by certain keys, permitted her as she wrote to hear the script being read in a jerky, male monotone.

Leonie tried to remember which keys to press in order to centralise the heading. Reward? Shift and F8 CE?

REWARD!

She needed to alert everyone, even those with a less altruistic nature.

LOST!

That was probably the next most important word.

A brown Burmese cat called Acajou wearing a green leather collar. Please contact ...

Then she changed her mind and deleted the name conjecturing that most people would not be able to pronounce it and he would be unlikely to respond to a stranger's voice in any case. Acajou is a peculiar name but it has a distinctive sound and as each cat would come when called, she had to choose clearly dissimilar names.

Acajou is a French word meaning mahogany and the dark sheen of his coat was reminiscent of that lustrous wood. The reasons for the choice of Suchard and Paprika were more obvious but there was still the colour link.

Leonie was gradually becoming more competent with the computer but had not yet learnt how to copy a block of print so, leaving plenty of space between each copy, she wrote out the advertisement four times, changed to the command mode and printed several sheets. At last, her Tuesday afternoons studying the computer and word processor with so many different key combinations were proving their worth. Little did she realise that she had failed to perform the correct ritual for centralising text and the top line read:

CE REWARD

The "CE" would have disappeared had she pressed just one more key. Janet, one of the neighbours who had offered to help earlier in the day, cut out the notices for Leonie as she could not be sure where each one started or finished and, armed with a large roll of sticky tape, together they set forth to adhere them to the road signs, the paddock fence and to the school gates. It was agreed that the "CE" would not matter.

As the school was about to break up for the half term holiday, Leonie felt there was an urgency to disseminate the news of Acajou's disappearance so they went into the school where a kind hearted secretary assured them that she would put up some notices herself and draw the children's attention to them before they left for the holiday.

Acajou must be hungry now not having been home for a meal for twenty-four hours and Leonie began to feel more convinced that he had been inadvertently shut in a garage or in a house where the family had gone away for the vacation. She knew that, if he were free, he would have made every effort to return home by this time.

At five o'clock, she prepared Toga's meal and cooked the fish for the cats but when she put her hands on the boiler to collect their plates, usually all empty by this time of day, a tear escaped. There was plenty of food left. Both the girl cats had lost their appetites and Acajou's share was untouched. She yearned for his return and even began to pray. She had always felt diffident about asking God for things that she wanted solely for her own pleasure. Need was one matter but to be allowed to indulge in sheer happiness was quite another. Leonie found the concept hard to grasp that God could care sufficiently and have time enough to help her to find Acajou. Every day, newspapers were full of calamities and only that morning she had been particularly moved by the appeal on the radio for peace made by the father of an eighteen-year-old soldier son who had been brutally murdered by the IRA. How could God possibly love every creature and have time to help her to find what was, after all, only a cat but, oh dear, such a loving and beloved one!

The doorbell rang. Leonie snatched a tissue from the box on the dresser, dabbed her eyelashes and, endeavouring to assume an air of composure, she hurried to open the front door. It was Joanna, a neighbour from Plymouth Place, whom she hardly knew and who had come with her two little girls, Helen and Mollie, to say that she had heard about Acajou and to see if there was any way in which she could help. Leonie was touched by her kindness; an offer to give her some time for which she would be so grateful.

Mollie was nine and a confident little girl, very sensible for her age and fond of animals. Helen, who was nearly seven and soon to become a Brownie, was only too keen to practise lending a helping hand. They discussed the various possibilities and agreed upon a plan of action. Joanna said that she would go down her road knocking on every door and ask people to look in their greenhouses, sheds and garages.

Leonie's spirits began to flag again. She could just imagine how perplexed Acajou would be, wondering why she had not come to collect him. He would sleep a lot, she supposed, but he would also just sit and wait expectantly. He had never been let down before and he would find it difficult to understand.

Suchard rubbed her head on Leonie's leg and she realised that she had not paid any attention to the other two cats. Each time another meal was due, Paprika would jump up on to the boiler where they were always fed and

Seeing is Deceiving

purr loudly in anticipation. The plates could not be put down on the floor as Toga was always ready to help to clear and polish anyone's dish.

When Andrew came home later in the evening, they decided to explore further afield after dinner even though it was now dark.

They tried to envisage an alternative scenario: If Acajou had been chased or if he, himself, had pursued another animal, possibly into the park, he could have become disorientated. Avoiding the risks of moving across large open spaces, he would have tried to find his way back to known territory walking amongst the bracken and keeping close to hedges and fences. So, even though it really was too dark to go looking in the park, they made their way along the High Street and down towards a group of houses built only recently for the elderly, with a view over the park as their main selling feature. A confused cat would surely wend his way eventually toward a cluster of lights and a place of human habitation. If he should emerge from the park at this spot, he would not recognise his surroundings. It was too dark for a satisfactory investigation and his name floated away through the night air unheeded. Before returning home, they checked the empty houses in their vicinity, creeping into the drives to stand and listen but there was no response to their whispered calls. The only cheering fact was that the weather was still warm and he would be able to hunt. Mice, voles and shrews had appeared on the rug in the hall from time to time, usually unblemished; no blood and no visible tooth marks. Leonie wasn't really sure that he understood about eating his prey. Perhaps hunger and natural instincts would overrule.

The cat flaps were left open all night but once again, the morning came and there was no Acajou.

Although it was Saturday, Andrew and Leonie arose

early and went to see if they could find their lost cat, looking for them perhaps? Was he off the beaten track on the other side of the hill in the park or even on the golf course? Small groups of deer were nibbling the thinning grass or crunching sweet chestnuts on the damp earth beneath the trees. Hearing a stag making extraordinary noises and, realising it was the rutting season, they took a detour to avoid upsetting or frightening them. It was then that Leonie heard it amidst the early morning polyphony. It was a faint mew in response to her attempted feline summons. Her heart leapt: At last! Lengthening their strides, they hastened in the direction of the sound that they had both heard. Leonie called once more and again, there was a timid answer but it was not quite the right pitch. By now, however, she was in the mood for clutching at straws. When the narrow path they were following emerged from the trees, Andrew saw, a few feet from the kissing gate that led out into the road, a red collared black and white cat rolling on his back in the autumn sunshine. Foolishly, Leonie toyed with the idea for a moment that Andrew's eyes might be deceiving him distorting the colours in the bright sunlight. In turn, they stroked the cat who purred with a rumbling pleasure. He, too, had probably lost his way but he was very near the gate and, rather than disturb his sense of direction or expose him to the hazards of the highway, they left him there to enjoy the glorious October morning. Walking home in silence past the vacant houses, Leonie pondered on Acajou's fate, the increasing lapse of time since he had been seen and his dependence on her for an alteration in the status quo.

Their younger daughter, Prudence, had left home for the first time at the beginning of the month to go to university and Leonie was becoming more acutely aware of her absence. If any one of their three children had been at home, he or she could have joined in the search and speeded its conclusion. However, as it was Saturday, there was shopping to be done and they set about their normal weekend tasks. At the supermarket, a trolley was filled with provisions for the next two weeks and Leonie wondered, as they loaded the tins of cat food which added variety to their diet, how many would be needed? Paprika and Suchard were unsettled and were not eating as much as usual. There was quite a lot of shopping to be done as they had been away in Ireland for a few days returning only on the Wednesday. An elderly lady, Miss Pepper, one of those old-fashioned and rare family treasures, had undertaken to keep house for them and to look after the animals, going home for two or three hours each day to have lunch with her twin sister. Now it was at lunch time that Acajou usually returned from his expeditions for a quick snack and a short respite, and to acquaint Leonie with his arrival, he would announce it with a loud utterance. The sound could be interpreted as a cat to cat communication but Leonie believed he understood that this audible salutation would alert her attention. In a veritably subservient manner, she would down tools and, after a few moments of low level aerial scanning with outstretched hands, she would find him and scoop him up in her arms. A nagging thought was haunting her: While Miss Pepper was caring for the three cats and they had been in Cork with Toga attending a conference, Leonie wondered if Acajou had become disenchanted with the lack of a midday greeting and migrated to kitchens new in search of a warmer welcome and perhaps a caress. She had planned to amend this state of affairs on the Thursday, the day after their return from Cork. In the morning, she worked at the hospital and there were several matters to attend to at home in the afternoon but in the evening, with the day's tasks completed, she hoped to spend time with the three cats who tended to take umbrage when they were away from home. It always took a little while to thaw their acquired icy reserve.

Against her better judgement, Leonie often showered the warmest welcome on the greatest wanderer, the most errant and prodigal of sons. Acajou strayed far further afield than the girls and she was always relieved to see him safely home again. He had a tomboyish appeal with his strident demands and an ability to tolerate rough games one moment and at the next expect comforting tenderness while draped over a shoulder or calmly curled on a lap. Would there be another chance to remedy matters or had he felt ignored, forsaken and sought solace elsewhere?

Noticing its vacant appearance, they decided to call that evening on the large house at the top of the hill whose extensive garden ran half way down the further side of Pine Hill Avenue. Its thick hawthorn hedge concealed well-kept lawns with a sundial and a rustic summer-house, immaculately tended flower beds and a mature apple orchard, part of which was devoted to the conservation of wild life and was full of intriguing mysteries for a curious cat.

Andrew rang the doorbell several times. There was a light in one of the windows but, as the same window only had been lit on the previous evening, they decided that it was probably activated by a time switch so, apprehensively, they opened the creaking side gate and made their way by the light of a torch around the side of the house. Leonie's husband did not enjoy this trespassing at all but she urged him on, conscious that in this quest no stone could be left unturned. The boiler house was locked but there was a tool shed whose door stood slightly ajar. Inside, there were boxes of hammers and chisels, jars of screws and nails, forks and rakes, a lawn mower and a huge bag of peat but no cat, nor was there any trace of one in the summerhouse.

It was then that they came upon the rainwater butt. It was about four feet in depth and, as Andrew leaned over to peer inside, Leonie suddenly felt sick. He was silent for a moment, probably concentrating, she supposed, and carefully focusing the torch.

"What is it?" she asked anxiously, "What have you found?"

"It's alright," he said, straightening up, "he's definitely not in there but as there was only about a foot of water in the bottom of the butt and it would have been impossible for him to climb up the side, I had to be sure. Come on," he continued, "let's go now. I don't like being on someone else's property uninvited."

Leonie knew the owners of the house vaguely and she was certain that they would not have objected to what they were doing and, had they been at home, they would willingly have helped. They were a hospitable couple and played host each year to the local residents' association carol singers. Gin and tonic, mulled wine and orange juice used to flow freely as gloved fingers were warmed before their blazing log fire. Mr and Mrs Duckworth had a young family of their own once and, in their latter years, they seemed to enjoy this brief reminder of bygone Christmas festivities.

Feeling somewhat emboldened by this excursion, Leonie persuaded her husband to go with her and have a quick look in the garden of the corner house in Lingham Way on whose wall the cats would take up their sentry duty. The little girl who lived there was very fond of Acajou and Leonie wondered if, after playing together, he had perhaps followed her indoors. This was indeed one of the places in which he could have been accidentally trapped. The family had only lived there for a year or two and she hardly knew them but she resolved to try and make contact. She had learned from Joanna that the father was frequently away and that the mother and her little daughter were going for a short holiday without him. If somehow she could discover where he worked she could ask him to come and look around the house for Acajou. Mr McCarthy was a strange, unfriendly person and even though Andrew had bidden him good evening once or twice when they met on the hill, he didn't speak. Unsmiling and with eyes averted, he would just jog on down to the gym where the Castleridge Harriers met on a Tuesday evening.

Before going to bed, Leonie spent some time with Suchard and Paprika. To find the cats when they were asleep was time consuming as she had to look in all their preferred places. First, she looked on the boiler top which was covered with a piece of carpet to reduce the heat and make a cosy spot for the cats. Then there were the chairs and sofa, of course, or the furry hammock that was suspended by its hooked frame from a radiator in the dining room. It took a while for Leonie to search as she had to feel gently for sleeping cats with her hands. Glancing in each room would have speeded this up but she did not like to distract Andrew from correcting his students' essays on his computer. He had already given up most of the evening to hunt with her for Acajou. Soon she found Suchard and Paprika in the hammock, uncharacteristically stretched out and relaxed as the third member had not come home to share it and crowd them all into a huddle.

Leonie retired to bed that night dissatisfied but at least she had decided upon the next course of action.

Meanwhile ...

Seeing is Deceiving

The engine was still running but the van was stationary with its door wide open. A light shone within and there was a faint smell of hay and freshly collected eggs. Whiskers aquiver, Acajou jumped down from his look-out post on the wall and crossed the grass verge to stand on his hind legs with his front paws on the van's step to investigate its interior. His view was blocked by a pile of cardboard boxes and not until he sprang inside could he see the rows upon rows of eggs stacked in trays, one above another. As he was peering into a particularly dark corner, the door was slammed behind him. He froze and, crouching low to maintain his equilibrium during the execution of a three point turn, he was dismayed to feel the vehicle going around the corner and jolting its way up the hill to the main road at the top. In rapid succession it lurched left, then right and left again negotiating two busy roads at the forked junction before stopping half way down another hill.

Chapter 3

Pins and Needles

On the Monday morning, after having put an advertisement in the "Lost and Found" column of the local paper, Leonie contacted Joanna who had taken the week off work in order to look after Helen and Mollie for the half term break. She was able to find the telephone number of the Running Club secretary who would have access to the members' addresses but, unfortunately, that proved to be a fruitless line of inquiry.

It was once again a pleasant morning and, before taking the children out to lunch as a half term treat, Joanna thought it would be fun for them to comb the immediate vicinity for Acajou. The two small girls regarded it as a kind of treasure hunt and, with permission from the various neighbours, they rootled through undergrowth, examined dark hiding places and clambered up fences to achieve a better height from which to scrutinise hollows in trees. They paid special attention to the McCarthy's garden which had been neglected of late and allowed to run riot. Hitherto highly prized, its soil was rich and untamed growth profuse. Weeds tangled with exotic plants and brambles choked the clematis and climbing roses that sprawled and straggled up and over the chestnut palings of the garden fence.

Joanna's kitchen window looked out on to Pine Hill Avenue and she had frequently seen the Kingsley retinue

Seeing is Deceiving

at the weekends on its way to the paddock led by Toga with the human attendants and followed by three Burmese cats usually in single file. This was how she had begun to know the family and she was always friendly and ready to talk when she met Leonie on the hill with Toga. Leonie had had three guide dogs: Grace, the first, was a beautiful cream labrador, who had arrived seven months after the birth of their elder daughter and lived up to all that was expected of an ever hungry, good natured and faithful labrador; a wonderful introduction to the world of guide dogs. Shep, the second one, who had died the previous winter, was a very pretty red sable border collie, not unlike a fox, even down to the white tip of her tail. The word "collie" will convey to any other collie owner the very special kind of relationship Leonie had with her. Whereas she loved and cared for her mischievous Grace, it was as another child in the family but Shep seemed to look after Leonie, guiding, guarding or shepherding as she thought necessary. Although she had undergone a rigorous training as a guide dog, her herding instincts were still strong and when the telephone or doorbell rang, she would ensure a speedy response by barking, nudging and general herding activity. She would also retrieve the various family pets in this way, one of the most elusive being the Belgian hare who used to have the run of the house in the evenings. Leonie recalled with admiration the strenuous efforts of a guide dog trainer to introduce Shep to the other pets when she first arrived and to teach her to respect or ignore them. He had to emphasise firmly and repeatedly that to chase the hare was a forbidden pleasure; amity was essential as Currant Bun, the hare, used to spend the evening in the sitting room with the family. He was completely house trained and, when nature called, he would leave his chosen spot underneath the piano to hop out of the sitting room, turn right and right again and down a narrow passage to the cloak room door behind which there was his own special sand filled Swiss roll tin. His resting place beneath the piano was selected, Leonie thought, because of the pleasing vibrations from the bass notes. He used to take up his position as soon as one of the children started to practise. Acajou also enjoyed music but he preferred to appreciate it from the top of the piano and he, too, showed a predilection for the lower tones while gently gnawing the corner of the lid that protected the strings. Currant Bun, the hare, alas, became a victim to modern farming methods. If, in the evening, Leonie were to eat a banana, he would hop up onto her lap and nibble the dangling skin. She was unaware at that time of the potent pesticides, fungicides and growth substances used on fruit and she was mortified and riddled with guilt when, one day, after having consumed a larger than usual piece of banana skin, he became ill. The vet gave Leonie some medicine for him which she tried to administer with an eyedropper but, being unable to see, it was all rather difficult and within three hours, he died leaving a very lonely guinea pig with whom he shared his hutch.

As it was Monday, Leonie had a hasty lunch in order to catch the 1.35 pm. train to Craybridge where, each week, she attended a sewing class arranged especially for blind and partially sighted students. It was held in the adult education centre. In a moment of enthusiasm, she had bought herself some rather expensive Cashmere woollen material with which to make herself a suit so she felt constrained to continue attending the classes and complete the extravagant project. Although from a distance the colour of the material, she was assured, resembled that of a shelled hazel nut flecked with green, it was, in fact, made up of tiny violet, green and oatmeal checks and sighted assistance was required for the precise matching of these when the pattern was being pinned on to the cloth.

The train journey took just over ten minutes and for a while, her mind and hands were occupied preventing Toga from hoovering beneath the seats, delving into empty crisp bags or trying to detach chewing gum from the floor with her front teeth. When disembarking, Leonie also had to be particularly alert as they walked along the platform lest her rascally dog should neglect her duties for a moment in pursuit of a pigeon, many of whom were also interested in the litter and discarded food. Sometimes, Toga had a tendency, too, to following ladies in fur coats but, as already mentioned, the weather was unduly clement and it was not a problem that afternoon.

As she turned left out of the station, Toga made an impulsive movement which Leonie recognised as the allure of yet more provender. Instructing her to "leave", she swooped at speed to raise her head from the ground, unclench her teeth and with her thumb she flicked from her mouth the tempting delicacy; this time half a roll filled with tuna. Before continuing on her way to the Adult Education Centre, she paused to take a paper handkerchief from her handbag with which to restore her thumb to its former fishy free state.

For the next two hours Leonie tried to concentrate on the assembly and machining of the skirt lining. A dear elderly lady who used to go to the class as a helper had already selected a sewing machine for her and set it out on a table. Having checked that she was about to use the appropriately coloured cotton, Leonie filled the spool and threaded the needle on the machine. This was quite simple with the aid of a commercially produced needle-threader. She then screwed on the seam guide 1.5 centimetres from the needle and positioned the unruly green taffeta in preparation for stitching. As she pressed the pedal with her foot, and studied the passage of material that slid beneath her fingers, she was able for a while to dispel the haunting image of a bewildered cat puzzled by the days of continuing neglect.

While Leonie sewed, Toga lay peacefully in the corner tethered to the radiator by her elongated lead. There was another guide dog that came to the class, a golden retriever, and, although she was gentle and compliant, she, too, was anchored in order to eliminate the possibility of confrontation, jolly or otherwise, between the two dogs. In actual fact, their behaviour when together was quite exemplary.

There were eight students in the class the average age of which was about sixty and dress size, large. This latter piece of information Leonie gleaned from snippets of conversation overheard when the suitability of a pattern was being discussed. There were four or five helpers who eagerly offered assistance but at no time were they permitted to take over the actual creation of a garment.

Seeing is Deceiving

The class instructor used to insist that the students did all the work because, she maintained, only then would there be a real sense of achievement and pride in the completion of a piece of work.

Six of the class members had a reasonably useful degree of vision and for them, the colours of cloth and thread were carefully studied. For example, orange or yellow thread was often chosen for stay stitching and making tailor tacks for these colours, provided the material was not of a similar hue, seemed to be clearly visible to a partially sighted seamstress. If anyone was very keen to be independent, the advice was to buy a monochromatic fabric as this avoided the problem of pattern placing and design matching. The first skirt that Leonie had made was in a plain navy-blue woollen fabric the surface of which was slightly coarser on one side than the other and she could even feel the direction of the grain. It was, indeed, easy for her to work with it with very little help. Later, having become somewhat over confident and having been lured to a sale at Liberty's by her elder daughter, she bought some

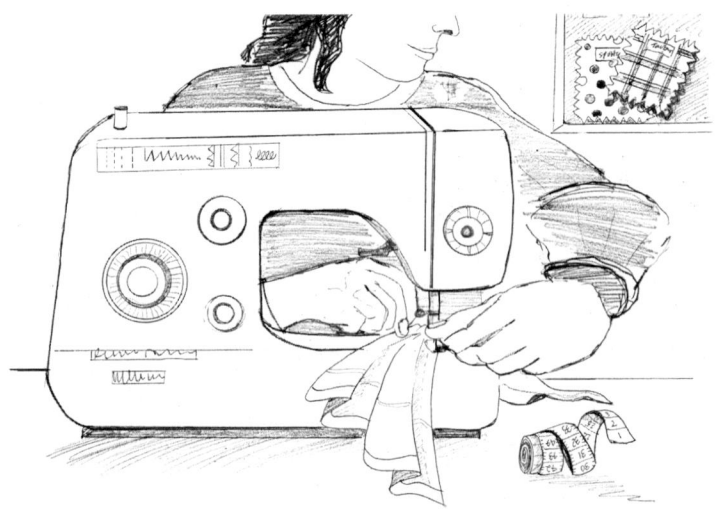

exquisitely fine red woollen material with a floral design. To make a dress from this required guidance with placing of the pattern and expert help to enable Leonie to produce a dress with symmetrically aligned flowers.

The paper, from which the patterns were made, was tissue thin and, on a similarly smooth cloth, particularly for an elderly student, it was not easy to feel the tiny holes for the insertion of tailor tacks that would mark the darts and gathers. The teacher overcame this problem by reproducing the pattern in a tougher substance such as parcel wrapping or inexpensive wallpaper. It was much easier to direct the scissor blades to the firm edge of a wall paper template than to a flimsy tissue paper margin.

There was another woman in the class who was, like Leonie, totally blind and they would often laugh and compare notes with one another about the inadequacies of finger-tip vision. Even Morag, a teacher with saintly patience and nerves of steel, sometimes flinched when she watched them at work, the seeing finger separated from the needle on occasions by a mere millimetre. There was, indeed, the odd incident when the needle passed through a finger nail controlling the insertion of a zip, an operation that required the use of a less protective single foot on the sewing machine. Leonie and Edith chuckled when they heard one or two ladies with a good helping of residual vision complaining about the indistinct markings on the temperature gauge of the steam iron when poor old Edith, still adjusting to her recent blindness, could not even find the ironing board, let alone the iron and its gauge without barking her shins on a stool or chair on the way across the room or singeing her fingers on arrival.

Spattering the material with spots of blood was another complication to be avoided and pin pricks were a common occurrence. When blood is freshly shed, the time when it is simplest to remove, digital detection is impeded by the fact that the blood is much the same temperature as the finger tip that it has just left. In essence, wet blood is not easy to feel. Variations in temperature as well as texture help a blind person to recognise what is being touched. Once, Leonie almost ruined a blouse that she was making from silk brought all the way home from China while completing the final button hole which activity took a fair amount of concentration. In order to create button holes of an identical size, it was necessary to listen to the machine as it sewed and to count the stitches while guiding the material with one hand and controlling a rotating knob with the other. Leonie had failed to notice a brief encounter with the point of a pin marking the width of the button hole. However, the blemish was soon noted by a vigilant helper and, with the aid of a sponge and some cold water, the situation was hastily remedied.

The sweet natured woman who usually helped Leonie was seventy-eight years old and profoundly deaf. She was at one time a matron in a boys' school in Tonbridge and, although she did not know a great deal about sewing, she was intelligent and observant, ever ready to give her guidance, to read instructions and to watch when Leonie was performing a tricky task to ensure that no drastic errors were made. Although Mary was frail and thin with bowed shoulders, she was happy to stand beside the cutting out desk without a single word of complaint. She had many problems of her own at home and Leonie thought perhaps that helping with the class enabled her to forget them for a while. Mary had two daughters, one of whom had just learned that she was suffering from multiple sclerosis. As she and her husband lived with Mary, she had shared in the agonising experience of acceptance. The diagnosis was made in June and just one week later, on the third of July, her son-in-law died of a heart attack while watching the television news after a routine day at work. He was only fifty-one and would have been the main stay in his wife's new life with a progressively crippling disease. In spite of all this, Mary never grumbled. She used to smile and greet Leonie with apparent pleasure when she arrived at the class with Toga so Leonie felt that the least she could do on this Monday afternoon was to talk to Mary and to work not mentioning her own anxiety which would seem so trivial in comparison with hers. Acajou was, after all, only a cat but how she loved and missed him!

She squashed the lump in her throat by swallowing the mug full of strong tea provided for the class by Gwen.

Morag, the teacher, was a delightful person, an intelligent woman with a keen sense of humour. She treated every new problem as a welcome challenge to overcome.

"You are right," she would say, "it's tricky sewing a straight dart if you can't see the tacking stitches and it is hard to follow an imaginary line from pin to pin but no one is going to do it for you so we'll just have to think of another way forward."

Five minutes – and the problem was solved. A piece of cardboard with a straight edge pinned in line with the tacking provided an excellent guide and the dart was completed with stitching as straight as a dye.

"Very satisfactory."

Morag was economical with praise but always ready with a quick smile and words of encouragement. Any signs of flagging endeavour or mild dejection were met with the teasing threat of a slap on the wrist. She was firm with the class expecting a high standard and always scrupulously fair with the division of her precious time for supervision and assistance. Morag was, Leonie suspected, a slightly eccentric lady and she had created for herself one or two startling outfits to be worn when she wished to be flamboyant. Even the more traditionally elegant clothes she made for herself had a touch of defiance about them. At the end-of-year party, she showed Leonie a smart silk suit that she had made for herself pointing out the intricately fabricated square petaled rose designed to perch on the shoulder but Morag had stitched it to the back of the neck. It was, however, still an attractive outfit and appealingly different. Her needle work was exquisite and judging by the reaction of those in the class with sight, her clothes always suited her and she looked immaculate. She was full of fun and optimism and she told them once how she had persuaded a friend to paint a huge bright yellow daisy on the garage door of her new tiny town house to remind her of the beautiful garden and the happier days she had left behind with her husband, his new girlfriend and her old home in the countryside.

No real chattering was encouraged in the class time but, over the mid-afternoon mug of tea, the students would exchange confidences, doubts and suggestions helping each other by sharing the ways in which they coped with sight deprivation. Most of them had only recently become handicapped by the problem and it was interesting to hear of the adapted machines and gadgets that improved the quality of life.

Lily, the butcher's wife, described the luminous orange paint-like substance retailed by the Royal National Institute for the Blind. It was garishly bright and visible by people with severely deficient vision. She told them that she had painted a stripe on the end of every saucepan handle so that its position on the stove was clearly discernible. Joan, a retired ward sister, talked about her new sense of independence now that she had a speaking weighing machine. The ravages of over indulgence were once again her own secret. She was also "tickled pink" by her talking wrist watch and "to death" by a talking clock whose alarm mimicked the crow of a vigorous young cockerel. However, she waxed truly lyrical in her praise of the liquid level indicator with its two parallel prongs that hooked over the side of a cup or glass and its shrill squeal when it came in contact with the liquid. It even possessed the refinement of two longer prongs to serve those who liked to add milk to the tea when a less full cup was required. Some could pour a drink successfully by just listening to the change in the sound but a quiet environment was needed to ensure accuracy. They all agreed that the finger-tip dip could not be used when the vicar called!

Most members of the class had heard about Braille, a reading system in which the letters are represented by raised dots but not one of them, other than Leonie who had lost her sight in an accident at the age of six, had bothered to learn it as it is fairly difficult to master if taken up in the latter years. However, it was refreshing to hear of the pleasure with which other ways of adapting to daily life were viewed.

Lily had been given for her birthday a rain warning device. "Mind you," she chortled, "I know old Sam meant well but, if I go outside, I get wet. I can feel them drops, no trouble at all. Kind thought though, wasn' it? It's a bloomin' piercing screech!"

Lily obviously thought that Leonie's favourite gadget was equally fanciful. It was a small pen shaped instrument the point of which was light sensitive. It measured light intensity by responding to the brightness of a light with a high pitched signal, the tone of which descended as the light was dimmed. This could be admirably demonstrated by pointing the tip towards a sunlit window and then to the curtains. Leonie used it at the physiotherapy clinic to

Seeing is Deceiving

check the functioning of certain machines. For example, the correct position of the electrodes on a short-wave diathermy machine, was indicated by a flashing light on one of the dials. The intermittent bleep from the light sensor which coincided with the flash impressed the patient and could add a science fiction dimension to the effectiveness of the treatment being administered. There was another piece of equipment designed especially with audible monitoring but this was less spectacular. At home, Leonie used the light sensor to check on the oven temperature and also to check whether or not the family members had left the lights switched on when leaving home for the day. In the winter when the mornings were dark, the younger members tended to leave with the house ablaze and it saved Leonie having to climb on to the edge of the bath in order to feel the temperature of the light bulb. When a light is controlled by a cord with a toggle switch, there is no means of checking the state of play. The light detector was also handy for testing the tree lights at Christmas.

Most of the ladies had a Braille tape measure, pins with brightly coloured heads and, for hand stitching, either a small gadget to guide the cotton or self-threading needles the eyes of which have a minute spring clip. The needle end is pressed against a taut thread which then slips obligingly into place. It is possible to thread an ordinary needle without sight if the end of the cotton is located with the tip of the tongue as the fingers steer it through the eye and it can then be pulled through with the teeth.

At the Christmas party held each year in the Adult Education Centre, everyone was required to wear her own hand made outfit. Note the subtly distinctive adjective on which Morag insisted. The word "home-made" she maintained, gives a very different impression from "hand made." She checked, too, that compliments would abound from the other members of staff and all the ladies left for home thrilled with their creations and full of confidence.

At twenty past three, on the dot, dear Mary would begin to gather up Leonie's scattered belongings hoping to speed up her effort to catch the three fifty-seven train back to Castleridge. She preferred to travel on that one as the next train was always filled to overflowing in the term time with school children.

As Leonie handed in her ticket on arrival, she shivered a little; the temperature was falling increasing the urgency for the retrieval of her beloved Acajou. She walked rapidly with Toga all the way up the chestnut tree lined avenue and along the main road towards the Memorial Gardens where she paused to call his name. She was anxious to reach home quickly ever hoping to be in time for that longed for phone call.

Toga had been well trained and she had learned to work at different speeds. She could guide slowly and carefully in a crowded shopping precinct or on the command "let's go" more swiftly only to change in to yet another gear if Leonie was late for an appointment when she would even run for a short distance but this was a little risky. Toga, however, seemed to be able to understand and to comply with Leonie's wishes. Slipping her fingers up her left sleeve, she pressed the catch on her watch. The lid sprang open. It was later than she had imagined but there would still be enough time to prepare the evening meal.

Chapter 4

Rather Fishy

Having taken the short cut through the Memorial Gardens, Leonie paused at the cobbled crossing but there was a helicopter hovering over the cricket ground and it was difficult to hear the traffic so she continued to stand at the edge of the kerb. It would have been impossible to hear a bicycle. A kindly passer-by asked her if she was having trouble with the dog but Leonie just smiled, amused by the response there might be if she mentioned the aircraft, and accepted the offer of a well-intentioned tourniquet grip above the elbow as she was propelled across the road. She had been in this situation before and had made the foolish mistake of trying to explain her reasons for the prolonged hesitation after which there was a short silence and the feet had walked away. The wintry gale was having a particularly violent moment on this occasion obscuring most of the traffic sounds.

As Leonie and Toga reached the final corner on their homeward trip, there was a scuffling sound in the recess at the top of the sandstone wall as Suchard and Paprika jumped down to greet her. This wall was an alternative observation post. Toga stopped and Leonie stood still so as to avoid treading on little paws while Paprika brushed her head against her trousers. Leonie bent down to stroke her before stretching out her hand to find Suchard whom she knew would be standing just a little way from her. She was more timid but Leonie knew she, too, was waiting for her caress.

Having removed Toga's harness and lead, Leonie opened the side gate and sent Toga through into the garden to relieve herself while she made her way to the front door along the narrow path and past the forsythia hedge. The phone shrilled and with trembling fingers, Leonie fished the keys from her pocket, selected the one without an identifying nick on it and opened the door as fast as she could before the phone stopped ringing. She was just in time but it was only Andrew to say that he would be late home. His thoughtfulness always touched her and she loved his rare calls but she was hoping for a cat contact.

Later there were two calls; one from a friend enquiring about Acajou but the second from a Mrs Judith Roberts who had seen the little yellow notice on a lamp post near her house and was wondering if it was the cat that came into her garden to watch the fish in her pond for at least five minutes earlier in the afternoon. Leonie took her address and, capturing Toga to prepare her for work again, they left at once to go back up the hill and through the Memorial Gardens to cross the road and search for number 14, St Mary's Drive. She found the approximate area and then stood still listening for approaching feet in order to discover the exact location of number fourteen. It was not long before a pair of high heels came up the hill and a cheerful young lady asked if she could help. Leonie was by number ten but was confidently guided by the wrist to the appropriate gate. When they were on their own once more, Leonie slipped her hand along the wooden bar across the top of the gate and found the latch pretty quickly. As she and Toga approached, the front door opened and a pleasant woman who said she had seen a cat come while watering her plants on the sitting room window sill. She wondered if it was the one described in the notice about the lost cat.

"It was dark brown or black," she said, "but when I moved the curtain to see more clearly, it ran off and I have not seen it since. That was about half an hour ago."

Leonie thanked her and turned to go home, quietly calling his name once more when she heard the door shut behind her. The silence was broken only by the melancholy cry of a ringdove. Blinking away a tear, Leonie swallowed hard and scratched Toga reassuringly behind the ears before closing the gate.

It was very late for the feeding ritual. In the garage, Leonie put a handful of biscuits from the plastic food bin into Toga's bowl and picked up a tin of dog food from the shelf beneath the window. She then selected a large piece of frozen coley from the freezer for the cats. Foolishly defiant, Leonie resolved to cook the same amount of coley as usual. She bought the fish by the stone in weight from a local fishmonger who delivered it in a frozen block that had to be thrown on to the concrete garage floor several times before it could be persuaded to yield up all its square segments. She always cooked it in a polythene bag in the microwave adding a sprig of eau de Cologne mint plucked from the herb tub beside the back door to counteract the piscatorial emmission! Two tablespoonfuls of water having been added, the polythene bag was placed in the microwave to be steamed on full power for six minutes. With the kitchen doors closed and the windows wide open to restrict diffusion of the odour in the house. The smell was minimal in comparison with that produced by the conventional method of cooking. The herbs which were on top of the bag of fish made an enchanting fragrance that successfully pervaded the kitchen. As a final precaution against the offensive smell, the fishy parcel was unwrapped in the garden and its contents cooled and served in the fresh air.

Rather Fishy

The polythene bag was discarded eliminating the tedious scrubbing of sticky fishy pans. The wind borne scent had a magical effect upon the cats that used to appear from nowhere and line up on the boiler top.

In order to accommodate their various personalities, food had to be served in three separate dishes. Paprika, for example, was prone to over indulgence and she seemed to think that the plate, however full, had to be left spotlessly clean. Suchard, on the other hand, had a small appetite and the most remarkable manners. Unless cajoled and invited to eat from her own special dish, she preferred to wait until the other two cats were satisfied before she would begin her meal. Summoned by the aromatic invitation, the two girl cats arrived but no Acajou and as Leonie gently stroked them both, a tear spilled into the unattended dish.

Lindsay from the top of Pine Hill Avenue telephoned to ask if Leonie had had any luck and to tell her that she had damaged her Achilles tendon while playing tennis in the morning. They discussed treatment for it and she said that her husband Simon had come home early from work and would be glad to go with her to the house opposite to help search for Acajou in the garden. Not only was Leonie anxious about trespassing on private property, particularly when alone, but she was also unacquainted with the geography so gratefully, she accepted the offer. Simon, who was rather shy and obviously unaccustomed to escorting a visually impaired person, bravely grasped her by the arm. To try and make him feel more relaxed, Leonie joked with him suggesting that it might be simpler if she were to take his arm so that he could be the first to fall down any unexpected holes or steps. He did not laugh. A good deal of unspoken information can be gained by this method of guidance as the sighted person is slightly ahead. His children, Colin and David, went with them but the ivy covered house was silent and in the fading daylight, it was not easy to see anything in the disorganised garden.

The following morning, after yet another dawn sortie with Andrew, she set off with Toga to walk through the town to the hospital.

As Leonie donned her white coat in the staff changing room where bits of news were exchanged and the staff discussed the coming alterations in the NHS, she mentioned Acajou's disappearance and her colleagues were sympathetic. She was told two or three encouraging stories of cats that had disappeared for days or weeks on end and returned with not a hair out of place. The receptionist, who had had a less fortunate experience, offered to phone the council on her behalf to see if the refuse officers had come across any corpses in the last few days.

"Refuse!!" The word made her shudder but she agreed that it would be far better to know of his fate.

The morning was busy and an hour had elapsed before Leonie was able to ask an aide to keep an eye on her patient who was having Curapulse, so that she could slip away to the receptionist's office, heart pounding, to see if there was any news. She was relieved to hear that no dead cats had been found. Bridget kindly agreed to look up some telephone numbers for her so that she would be able to make more inquiries from home at lunch time. On the pocket recorder used for taking patients' histories, she noted numbers for Radio Kent, Invicta Radio, the RSPCA, the police station and the local pet shop.

The automatic timer set for Mrs Thorpe buzzed as she walked down the corridor back to the department. When explaining to her patient what she had been doing, Mrs Thorpe generously offered to take some of her notices and to stick them on gate posts and trees in her road. It was somehow comforting to talk to her about Acajou and

Rather Fishy

to answer her questions on the topography of his routine patrols. Owning a dog and two Persian cats herself, she seemed genuinely keen to help. Leonie confided her fond hope that someone somewhere might find him sheltering in a porch or even entering a kitchen, drawn by tempting smells and the anticipation of a warm greeting. In this imagined scenario, the finder would stoop to read the telephone number on his identity disk and make contact without delay. Happily, most patients are so interesting and have such varied stories to tell that the morning soon passed.

Her last patient was a new one; a lorry driver who had been attacked by armed thugs in Southwark. They had stolen half his lorry load but, he added with some relish, they would have difficulty in flogging the loot as the load consisted of tubular metal chair frames, all of which were substandard and being returned to the factory. He had been admitted to Guy's Hospital for a couple of days and now he was being treated as an outpatient at the Castleridge Clinic for a back injury.

While Leonie treated the extensive bruising with ultra sound and ice, he entertained her with diverting tales about his job. One anecdote was concerned with the dubious way in which meat was labelled.

"I drive the old lorry to Northern Ireland," he told her, "where I pick up a load of beef, Irish beef, you understand, from a small town near Belfast. Then I take the boat back to Liverpool, drive all the way across England to Dover, get on to the ferry for Calais and drive on to Paris where one of the carcasses is unloaded, one of the best, of course. A French inspector examines and stamps it as fit for French consumption. The carcass is then reloaded and I drive all the way back to Smithfield where the whole lot is sold as French beef! The fiddles would amaze you," he continued. "Now take coffee, for example, there is some EEC tax-dodge there. I collect a load of instant coffee, a well-known brand from Milton Keynes, take it on the boat from Harwich to Rotterdam, drive off the boat down the road to the first roundabout and back again to Milton Keynes so that some duty or other imposed by the EEC can be avoided. Hey presto, increased profit for someone!"

As Leonie hurried home with Toga at lunch time, still anxious about any telephone calls that might have been missed, the idea suddenly came to her, an answer-phone! This would enable her to go out searching without missing any vital messages. If only a phone to be carried in a pocket could be invented!

At the gate, Leonie was greeted in the customary manner by Suchard and Paprika. They complained bitterly about her absence and while the former wound herself around her legs, the latter liked to sharpen her claws on the gatepost. She often wondered how long they spent just watching and waiting for her. Sometimes they sat and waited between the battlements of the high Kentish ragstone wall that enclosed the garden of the corner house on her side of Lingham Way built by the council in compensation for the strip of land that was taken when Pine Hill Avenue was widened. Hawthorn hedge and old man's beard was uprooted and the grassy bank was levelled and replaced by an asphalt path.

Leonie stroked Suchard and Paprika before taking Toga to go to her special corner of the garden and then, after a cube of cheese, a banana and a cup of coffee, she made all her phone calls including one to British Telecom to order the installation of a new telephone with an answering machine. The customer adviser told her that she would have to go to a shop in Tunbridge Wells to select the appropriate model. Leonie mentioned the circumstances of her disability, quite useful on these occasions, and it was agreed that an answer-phone would be put in the van on November the fourth, the earliest date that could be offered for the installation.

The Radio Kent reporter sounded sympathetic and assured her that he would be only too pleased to include her request in the pet feature that was put out every afternoon between four and five o'clock and he added that the "Lost and Found" spot frequently produced very good results. He sounded so cheerful that Leonie was tempted to feel optimistic but as she could rarely listen to the radio during the afternoon herself, she wondered how many other people living in the vicinity would do so. Invicta Radio agreed to broadcast her appeal but said that it would only be broadcast once whereas the Radio Kent reporter had intimated that the item could be repeated several times if necessary.

The man in the pet shop told her that he was willing to display a notice in his window but he could not accept the details by telephone.

Seeing is Deceiving

    The police were distinctly disinterested and said that cat deaths were not even recorded.

    Suchard and Paprika trouped in through the cat flap tunnel and leapt up on to the boiler suggesting that a few biscuits would be welcome so Leonie found the box of cat biscuits in the pet cupboard and sprinkled some on two small plates before going into the garden to call Toga – no response! Oh dear! She had left it too long and she had probably gone to the far end to rummage through the compost heap before sneaking through the only remaining gap in the fence damaged by the famous gales in October of 1987. As she crossed the lawn to the steps which led up between the steep banks of heather to another lawn and vegetable garden, she heard a tinkle, a cat bell. Her pulse quickened. She called but she knew in her heart that it was not the correct note – it must have been the Siamese next door. All her cats wore collars with bells but each with a different sound so that she was able to recognise its owner en passant. The collars were made in differing fabrics and with just a fleeting touch, she could tell who was who. The cats did differ in shape and size, of course: Paprika had a slight tendency to portliness and her fur had a mildly fluffy quality. Suchard had a kink in the very tip of her tail and Acajou was the largest of the three but, when many legs and three tails were woven into a comatose tangle, it seemed a shame to disturb them by measuring girths or unfurling tails so one velvet, one suede and one smooth leather collar afforded speedy identification. Leonie did not call again but the owner of the bell did not speak and she returned to her original mission which was to retrieve Toga.

    She crossed the upper lawn with one hand raised to head height in order to ward off an unyielding branch of the Bramley apple tree remembering not to give it too wide

Rather Fishy

a birth lest she should be arrested by the trailing thorns of a Sealing Wax rose which had been trained to disguise and to climb all over a rather aged and rusty climbing frame.

At last Leonie heard the chink of a larger heavier bell as Toga nosed her way along the hedge of the adjacent garden endeavouring to find the hole through which to slink home and stand by the back door with head hanging and tail between her legs. She was admonished before being taken into the kitchen to have her nose and paws thoroughly washed as they reeked of well ripened compost.

Chapter 5

No Mouse? The Technical Approach

On alternate Tuesday afternoons, Leonie went to a school for blind and partially sighted youngsters where Mr Branson, a specialist teacher, taught her how to use an Opticon and a computer with added software which was able to convert the printed word into speech. Key strokes had to be learned for every activity as the mouse could not be used without vision.

The Opticon was a reading device for blind people. It had a minute camera which helped to transform an image on the printed page into a tactile configuration. Varying

No Mouse? The Technical Approach

numbers up to 124 tiny pin points beneath a finger plate housed in the main body of the machine raised electrical stimuli which replicated the exact formation of the letter on the page. With the index finger of the left hand resting on the finger plate while the right hand manoeuvred the minuscule camera, it was possible, at a pretty snailish pace, to read script if it was of sufficient size and clarity. Leonie decided that a thriller read at her speed would induce a coronary catastrophe or, at least, tachycardia in someone prone to that condition. The invention of the Opticon has been an exciting and major step forward in the development of technical aids for blind people but it was extremely expensive and, therefore, owned by very few individuals. She found it thrilling to learn to read with an Opticon and being loaned one of the school machines for a few months gave her an extraordinary new sense of independence. She had not yet learned to read hand writing but, as she had been without sight since early childhood, she was having to learn the various forms of personalised hand writing. When Leonie was seven years old, her mother used to while away the long train journeys to the boarding school at the beginning of term by teaching her to do joined up writing with thin Plasticine worms. The Opticon had several limitations, however, one of which was its inability to read the dot matrix system script produced by many computers and their printers. After an hour with the Opticon, Leonie studied simple computer programming and the use of the word processor.

As she switched on the kettle later that afternoon, she tried to suppress mounting excitement. If contact could be made with Mr McCarthy at the Athletic Club, she might at last be able to free Acajou. He would be so hungry by now, frightened and confused; disappointed she had not come to collect him and wondering why she had forgotten him.

Leonie selected a piece of smart writing paper and composed a letter to Mr McCarthy. She wanted to convey a sense of urgency and to interest him in wishing to help without offending or appearing to be presumptuous. Joanna's offer to come for her at six o'clock to take her to the gymnasium was most welcome and she arrived promptly with her two children. She told Mollie to take Leonie by the hand explaining that, without a dog, it would be more difficult for her to find her way. As she slipped her small hand into Leonie's, Mollie seemed to be a little worried by the responsibility of having to guide her and Helen tentatively took her other hand. Leonie joked with them about having never before been looked after by two guide dogs at once. They giggled and the tension was gone. They chatted about the impending Halloween, apple bobbing and transforming turnips into lanterns with strange faces. Then, as gripping fingers steered her carefully down a narrow little path to the Gymnasium, Mollie asked, "How on earth would Toga know where you wanted to go? She doesn't know the word Gymnasium, does she?"

Briefly, Leonie explained the way in which she worked.

"She understands the words Left and Right, Forward and Back and she stops at steps, up or down," she told them. "She prevents me falling down holes and walking into trees and lamp posts. To come here, we would have crossed the Avenue together and then I would have asked her to find the gate. After that, she would have led me down this narrow, windy path as far as the steps and," she added to their amusement, "believe it or not, she even points her nose in the direction of the door handle for me."

Helen giggled again and began to replicate this commendable refinement.

It was good to have Joanna with her for Leonie felt somewhat diffident when meeting people whom she

No Mouse? The Technical Approach

did not know at all and Joanna had a more confident and positive approach. Eye contact, she felt, facilitated introductions and it was an advantage to be able to make a quick visual assessment of the person to be addressed. Once he or she has spoken, Leonie could judge from where the voice was coming and accordingly, she was able to adjust the direction of her gaze. Failure to do this seemed to be disconcerting for many folk. Great importance is attached to facial expression but all kinds of clues can be picked up once speech has been triggered. Leonie was not skilled in the use of the more subtle eye signals and an intended wink could look more like a nervous tic. She used to laugh when her mother told her that perhaps she need not practise trying to flutter her eye lashes, should she wish to be flirtatious, as it looked more like an attempt to remove a speck of dust. However, Leonie found that by winking at Paprika, she could stimulate a long and noisy conversation.

When they reached the gymnasium door, it was locked. They were too early. Leonie thanked Joanna and the two little girls for their help and they returned home but Joanna kindly offered to take the letter for Mr McCarthy and said she might see him passing when working by the kitchen window.

Leonie peeled the potatoes and was putting the pan on the cooker when the telephone rang. As she ran to answer it, Toga barked and tried to race her to it as though infected by her mood of optimism. It was Joanna but the news was disappointing. She had tracked down Mr McCarthy who maintained that he did not possess a key now that he was separated from his wife. The cat, he said, could not possibly be shut in the loft of his own house which was near the gymnasium, a suggestion that Leonie had made in her letter, as his daughter was not allowed to go up there and the suitcases that they took away on holiday with them were all kept in the spare bedroom. She was partially relieved but also very disappointed. If he wasn't there, where was he?

Chapter 6

Cat Tales

Andrew, Leonie could see, was beginning to give up hope but, for her sake and in order not to compound her fears, he again rose early on the Wednesday morning and together they hunted further afield. On the way home, they met a neighbour from Plymouth Place who asked them if their lost cat had been found. His own large and handsome Burman cat had left home but been seen several times in the park. His wife had managed to find him and bring him home but he had enjoyed his wanderings so much that he left for the park again the following morning. He was still seen sometimes but he had never come home again. He told them he had heard about the cat and that Gemma, his fifteen-year-old daughter, had spent the previous morning riding her horse in the park and checking any undergrowth that might conceal an injured animal. Leonie was very touched; neighbours whom she hardly knew seemed to understand and were willing to help.

After lunch, she telephoned the vet to see if any injured cats had been brought into the surgery and then she rang the RSPCA. The duty officer assured her that there were no Burmese cats on his list but he gave her some useful telephone numbers. He suggested that Leonie should ring the Burmese Cat Register in Gloucestershire and an address in London, another outpost of the Burmese Cat Club. She was also given the names of two local cat lovers

Seeing is Deceiving

who might be willing to help and a third in Orpington who advertised in the local paper under the title "Cats Any Time!"

The name appealed to Leonie in her present mood so she dialled this number first.

A charming lady answered and, having listened attentively, she spoke to Leonie with genuine interest and commiserated before describing some of the escapades of her own seven cats, three of whom were Burmese. There were encouraging anecdotes about cats vanishing only to appear several days later without a satisfactory explanation, cats marooned at the top of trees and others shut in garages or lofts. There were a couple of more blood chilling tales, too, one of which involved a cat being holed up by builders in the foundations of a house and the other a thirteen-week-old kitten who had had an even closer shave. One of her friends, a nurse, had been stopped in her tracks one busy morning by the sound of her distressed kitten, a newly acquired lilac Burmese, who had only been with the family a week or so. Within seconds, she was

able to trace the mewing to the washing machine which she had switched on while clearing the breakfast table and opening the morning post. The water was still running into the machine and she had to wrestle with the door to break the safety device which prevented it being inadvertently opened before a washing programme had been completed. She hadn't dared to advance the programme to "Door Release" as this would have caused the drum to spin, but even this story had a happy ending. The door was eventually wrenched open and the kitten safely retrieved.

They discussed local breeders and discovered that one of their cats had an ancestor in common and then she concluded by suggesting that Leonie should get in touch with Cat Rescue, a charity set up by Celia Hammond, a former model who gave up her highly successful career in order to devote her time to the rescue of ill-treated, trapped, injured or unwanted cats.

Having obtained the telephone number from Directory Inquiries, Leonie contacted the nearest Cat Rescue Centre which was in Tunbridge Wells and was advised to speak to Celia Hammond herself in London.

Celia's voice was resonant and beautiful and she sounded as lovely as she must have looked in her days as a top model. She listened to Leonie patiently and seemed fully to comprehend the practical difficulties encountered by a blind person in search of a possibly silent animal. She suggested writing literally hundreds of notices asking people to look in their garages, garden sheds, greenhouses etc. and to deliver them to every house in the area frequented by Acajou plus those in which there might be news of a sighting in response to her newspaper advertisement.

"You must also get in touch with anyone you hear of who owns a brown Burmese cat," she said, "and if it wears a collar the same colour as Acajou's, ask them to change it

Seeing is Deceiving

just until he has been found and that will help to clarify identification. When he has been spotted," she continued, "do put food down regularly at that site, particularly at dawn and at dusk because that's when cats are on the move."

It was encouraging to hear that the chances were better of finding a cat with an unusual appearance.

"Black and white ones are so numerous," she explained, "that members of the public rarely report finding them for it is difficult to recognise who is the native and who the stranger. Generally speaking," she said, "owners give up searching too soon and consequently, there are colonies of feral cats all over the country."

Later that afternoon, Leonie turned on the radio, tuning it to the local station, to hear the daily feature on pets, lost and found. She felt hurt. The presenter sounded far too flippant; he talked about Acajou just as though he were a mislaid umbrella or briefcase. She thought it must have been noted by his supervisor because the following day the whole programme was far more sympathetic and the part concerning lost pets was introduced by a solemn sounding man called Clive. Obviously, it was not as easy as she had presumed for a producer to strike a happy medium.

Chapter 7

The Mystery Caller

There were no calls on Wednesday and Leonie feared that the trail might be going cold but in the evening, she took a taxi to the riding stables where there was always pleasure to be found. In her class, there were usually three other riders, all of whom had varying disabilities, none of which were severe. One had a partially paralysed left leg, one a curvature of the spine and the other, painful shoulders and a mild learning disability. Many riders at the RDA Centre, Riding for the Disabled, had more incapacitating problems. In her class, they were all able to trot, canter and even go over low jumps if they felt sufficiently confident. Leonie was the only one in that

class who was unable to see and she relied upon battery operated speakers that enabled her, for example, to trot at K, canter at C or stop at F. There were marked places around an arena and the eight most commonly used were A, M, B, F, A, K, E and H. The sensation of cantering at speed without a leading rein around an arena never failed to thrill; the exhilarating feeling of freedom combined with the joy of communication with the horse was wonderful!

Leonie's main hopes now were pinned on the *Castleridge Chronicle* which came into the shops on a Thursday morning. She checked her watch for the umpteenth time but it was only ten past seven. Soon, they would be putting the newspapers out on the shelves in W. H. Smith's.

The time now was palling and she could settle to nothing. It wasn't until a quarter past two in the afternoon that the telephone rang. She could have walked back from hospital with Toga rather than rushing to catch the bus home.

"Don't raise your hopes," the caller warned, "I just wondered if you had had any luck yet looking for your lost Burmese cat. I saw the advertisement in the paper."

Leonie told her no but she was none the less pleased that she had phoned, cheered to think that the column on pets was being read. "I have two Burmese cats of my own," she continued, "and they are such adorable creatures. I can't bear to think of one being lost. I will keep a look out for him and do let me know, won't you, if there is anything I can do to help. One of our cats is brown; he is called Kaftan and I thought I ought to tell you in case someone should see him after having read the paper and phoned you. It would be such a shame to raise your hopes falsely."

There was Leonie's opportunity and she asked her about the colour of Kaftan's collar. She was a little taken aback by this question so Leonie explained and she was assured that there could be no confusion there as his collar was red and she added that both her cats were rather timid, hardly venturing beyond the garden next door so there wasn't much chance of receiving a phone call about Kaftan. "However," she said, "I'll keep an eye open for him and do let me know, won't you, if there is any news at all."

Leonie promised and thanked her for her concern adding that she might be only too pleased to accept her offer of help. Light-heartedly, Leonie mentioned her predicament hoping that she would look out for Acajou even more enthusiastically on her behalf. There was a moment's silence followed by obvious recognition.

"I think I know you," she exclaimed, "you are Mrs. Kingsley! My husband is the bursar at Abbeyfield Hall School. I believe you had two daughters there, didn't you?"

They chatted for a further five minutes and Leonie began to feel quite cheerful, enjoying comparing notes about their charges in an addicted way, apparently common to so many owners of Burmese cats. It was fun to discuss their mutual infatuation.

There were no more calls until almost six o'clock in the evening. It was Joanna to say that she had been talking to a neighbour and heard about a van that delivered eggs locally every Thursday evening.

"I gather," she continued, "that he leaves the door wide open while calling on his various customers and I wondered if perhaps your cat had jumped in and been driven away. You said he had a tendency to do that sort of thing, didn't you?"

Leonie agreed and thanked her for the suggestion. She was thrilled; a lead at last! – A positive line of investigation. She was beginning to feel like a detective on "Crimewatch". There might be clues or even witnesses. It was late. She had to get organised. She might have missed the van already. The neighbour who had bought some eggs was a Mrs. Jones and, having extracted her number from Directory Enquiries with some difficulty – her husband's nickname, Curly, was of no importance to British Telecom – and it took a little while sifting through all the one hundred and one members of the Jones clan resident in Castleridge before alighting upon the correct address. Leonie discovered that the van's approximate time of arrival was half past six. It was at about this time last week, she mused, that Acajou had disappeared. She had always been aware of the risks attendant upon his freedom: his beguiling trust and insatiable curiosity made him vulnerable but, once the cats had reached maturity, she and Andrew had agreed not to curtail their liberty by day. A nocturnal curfew was imperative for their safety and no real hardship.

Leonie slipped into her pocket the mini-recorder, dressed Toga in her harness and hurried up the hill. Although it was a little early, she was not prepared to miss the egg van at any cost and its time of arrival might vary a little from week to week. Fortunately, the cool spell had passed and it was once again very mild.

At last, she heard the guttural vibrations of a diesel engine, probably a van, coming round the corner from the main road and, as it slowed down to park about ten yards away from her, she decided that this might be it. Toga eagerly responded to the instruction, "Find the van", for she well understood this command which featured prominently in her training. At the Guide Dog training school, the class, that consisted of eight dogs and their novice owners, set forth each morning to train in the busy streets of a local town.

To facilitate assembly, the van, driven by a guide dog trainer, was parked at a predetermined spot near the gate

The Mystery Caller

of the training centre. The young dogs enjoyed working and going for walks, so it was with pleasure and keen anticipation that they soon learned to obey the words, "Find the van".

The door of the egg van slid open as Leonie approached. The driver was polite and cheerful but obviously in a hurry to complete his rounds and he did not seem to be interested in the loss of a cat.

"No, I've not seen a brown cat but it's funny you should mention it; only the other day a cat did jump out just as I was opening up to load in the morning. Must have spent the night in the van. Fast as a bullet he was but he was mostly black with a bit of white on his face."

Black? A trick of the shadows and white on the face, egg white on this face – egg white acquired during the examination of the cargo?

"Cats often hitch a ride from me," he continued, "they must like the smell of the eggs and then there's the odd chicken feather, of course, free range, you see – probably tickles their fancy!" and he laughed heartily at his own witticism.

How many cats, she mused, became strays because of unplanned rides? The legendary homing instinct, contrary to general belief, rarely prevailed when a vehicle had been used for the journey. Quelling her over active imagination, and hastily dismissing a turmoil of thoughts, Leonie switched on the recorder in her pocket and asked the egg van driver if he would be kind enough to tell her which road he would visit next?

"Well now," he replied, his voice disappearing into the van, she was delaying him and he was in a hurry to get on. "Now," he continued as he emerged, arms probably filled with egg boxes, "St Mary's Drive first, then right down the hill and across the main London Road near the station, up Granville Road and along South Park, down those very steep roads, Crown whatever and Valley Drive, then right across to the other side of Castleridge," (her heart sank) "to the crescent; it's in the middle of that large housing estate near the boys' school."

"And after that?" she urged.

"Why then," he said, "straight on home to Farnborough. Plenty of work for one evening!"

Farnborough was about half an hour's drive from Castleridge. What chance had she of finding Acajou if he had stayed in the van until the end of its journey but he assured her that once he had got home to Farnborough, he would not unlock the van door until the morning when he would certainly see a brown cat if one was there. With that, he strode away, a gate clanged and he was gone.

While waiting for Andrew to come home, as the meal was already prepared, Leonie decided to write some more notices on her computer. She varied them a little designing some to appeal to children with the heading: TREASURE HUNT! These, she thought, would be more effective for distribution to schools and Joanna had offered to take some to Mollie's Brown Owl who would, she felt sure, be happy to hand them out at the end of their meeting. As she did not wish to shorten the time Andrew would have to continue the search, she tried to think who else she could ask to help cut up the sheets of notices in time for her husband to deliver some when they had finished their dinner.

Lindsay, such a warm, friendly smiling soul from somewhere in the north of England, where people seemed to grow up in an atmosphere of genuine neighbourliness, might ask one of her sons if they would like to earn some money. Leonie would gladly pay to have the notices delivered for her.

"Colin and David are both out," she said, "but don't

worry love, it'll be no trouble. You bring them up to me when you're ready and I'll see what I can do."

As Leonie separated the sheets of paper from the large block she used for the printer, she found that she had printed well over a hundred sheets; more than four hundred notices.

When Leonie called Toga to harness her yet again, she seemed to be a little perplexed and came to her rather reluctantly. How foolish she was! She felt her Braille watch and it was a quarter to eight, obviously dark and she had forgotten to switch on the light again. Andrew was rather late. She ought to leave now and she might meet him coming home from the station. They almost ran up the road to call on Lindsay first. Leonie had visited her with Andrew on previous occasions but this time, she hoped Toga might be able to locate the gate with just a little help. They walked over half way up the hill and Toga paused and sniffed. Leonie put out her hand and there were sharp thorns; this was it – George, Lindsay's husband, was renowned for his roses. Toga took another pace or two and then stopped. Success! And there was the wrought iron gate, a curving path, two steps and the door. Leonie found the bell and pressed it. Seeking any new destination with her guide dog always had a touch of adventure about it and, when successful, a sense of satisfaction.

Leonie knew the way to the egg van parking spot in the Drive and when she and Toga reached it, they paused and she called quietly to Acajou – but there was no sound, no movement in the hedge – so they walked on and met Andrew on the hill.

Although he was weary after a long day at work, Andrew soon recovered after their meal together and was ready to set off once again to continue their hunt for Acajou but this time in the car as they had a longer distance to cover.

Having collected the thick wodge of neatly trimmed notices, (Lindsay had telephoned to say that she had finished cutting them up for her) they drove up to the top of the hill, across the two busy roads at the forked junction and down St Mary's Drive where they made their first stop. While Andrew posted slips of paper through letter boxes and stuck some on to lamp posts, Leonie called and listened. It was yet another warm evening and there was a good chance Acajou might be out hunting for something with which to assuage his appetite. As they walked down one of the more deserted roads, Leonie called again, pausing to listen as they passed each garden but the disturbing sound in an otherwise peaceful night made Andrew wince so she curbed her enthusiasm and modified her efforts to communicate. They both used to converse with their animals at home stimulating vigorous vocal responses but, when out of doors, it was a different matter. Leonie laughed and said no more. Andrew was easily embarrassed when she behaved in an unconventional way. It was late. He was tired and she respected his natural sensitivity. He was so tolerant and patient to continue searching with her, night after night on what could be a fruitless errand. His male logic told him, she suspected, that cats do disappear and were frequently killed on busy roads. She was grateful for his consideration and the least she could do was to avoid irritation and to maintain a cheerful disposition, reserving her anxiety and tears for the night time when she was alone. She would creep out of bed into her daughter's empty room at two or three o'clock in the morning, when sleep eluded her, to toss and turn without disturbing Andrew and to listen to the radio to hasten the passing of the long night hours.

Montague Crescent, a large housing estate, was close to an extensive area of woodland which would, indeed, appeal to a cat. It was almost ten o'clock by then so they decided to come again for a more thorough search at the weekend in the daylight.

After breakfast, there was a telephone call from another *Chronicle* caller. She introduced herself as Barbara Young and asked if Leonie had found her cat before telling her about one she had seen.

"I was driving down St. Mary's Drive," she said, "when a glossy brown Burmese cat ran straight in front of the car. He came from the direction of that large white house. The garden was overgrown and the place looked uninhabited and is up for sale, I think, and he went towards the little road almost directly opposite. He was wearing a green collar too and, by the way, the number of the house is 57. I looked specially."

It all fitted in with the egg van story. Leonie was overjoyed and after having thanked her for being the harbinger of such marvellous news she asked her how long ago she had seen the cat.

"Wednesday – er, no Tuesday," she answered, "at about ten o'clock in the morning."

Leonie could not question too rigorously, of course, but she was curious to know why she had taken such careful note of every detail before having read the notice in the newspaper. It was also unusual that she was able to recognise a Burmese cat when she saw one. Most people mistake a feline form of that shape and shade for a Siamese and they certainly would not have remembered the collar colour or the house number. Leonie asked her if she would mind giving her address so that she could send her the reward but she only laughed saying that she wouldn't want it anyway. After apologising for not being able to offer any more help as she was not a resident of the town, having seen the cat merely while passing through, she concluded

Seeing is Deceiving

by wishing Leonie luck and rang off. Tuesday – and now it was Friday. Her description was so good that Leonie felt sure it must have been Acajou that she had seen. She had an authoritative tone of voice and, in spite of the anomalies, she sounded reliable. It was, nevertheless, strange how she had memorised everything with such precision when she was not in her own home town. If she did not live in Castleridge, why, she wondered, did she read the local paper? A journalist, perhaps, possibly a business woman or a school teacher – but a teacher wouldn't be driving down St Mary's Drive at ten o'clock in the morning? And then she remembered it could be half term, of course; some schools were later than others. Despite the fact that their two daughters had taken piano exams in that very house, number 57, Leonie and Toga were not really familiar with the geography of the area and a guide dog cannot attain a destination unless the owner is conversant with the intended route.

Leonie had two friends who taught in Abbeyfield Hall Junior School and she knew that, if at all possible, one of them would be willing to help her and she decided to contact them that afternoon.

It was getting late but it was with raised spirits that she called Toga and set off for the hospital. As the morning glory and the sunflower, so the local residents seemed to be affected by the bright sunshine, emerging from the tight budded privacy of their houses to bloom in their gardens; sweeping up leaves, clipping hedges or simply smiling and chatting over the fence. When returning home, therefore, Leonie did not like to call Acajou and just hoped Toga's bell might attract his attention and entice him from his secret retreat.

After lunch, it was time for some phone calls and she phoned Madeleine first. However, she was unable to

The Mystery Caller

come as she was looking after her frail and elderly mother but Faith said she would love to help and within half an hour, she was on the doorstep insisting that there could be nothing better than a walk on such a beautiful sunny afternoon.

Asking for favours was always difficult but when they were granted with such enthusiasm, it helped to dull the acute sense of indebtedness.

Faith and Madeleine jointly owned and dearly loved an elderly labrador who had originally been partially trained as a guide dog and had only failed to qualify because of her hypersensitivity. She was a little too nervous to take decisions when under stress. For example, if she encountered a large hole or a car parked on the pavement, a guide dog is trained to go to the kerb and then, to await instructions to be obeyed only when the road is clear. When traffic permits, on the bidding "Forward" the dog guides the owner along the road to regain the safety of the pavement as soon as the obstruction has been bypassed. If traffic is still thundering past on the opposite side of the road, it is difficult for the blind person to hear and to make a wise judgement and if the dog lacks courage, the duo would be indefinitely delayed. In actual fact, all guide dog owners are cautioned to take sighted assistance whenever danger threatens.

Faith and Madeleine were both fond of Toga and sometimes took her for walks when Leonie and Andrew went abroad on holiday, leaving the menagerie in the care of their elderly Miss Pepper who was more short sighted and less sure footed than she used to be. So, it was with a rumbustuous welcome that Toga greeted one of her favourite visitors.

Leonie did not bother with the harness as she would be walking with Faith but she did put on her play collar with

Seeing is Deceiving

its bell as it was to the sound of this that Acajou seemed to respond. It also enabled Leonie to keep an ear on all her activities. Toga had a tendency to join in with cat frivolity and as she was a big dog and heavier than all the cats put together, it was occasionally necessary for Leonie to intervene and lower the temperature when she became too excited and entered the mad chase, racing around the house. A swaying tail, a playful nip or a provocative dab could trigger the thunder of flying feet as fugitive and followers streaked up the stairs, under the beds and through a maze of chair and dressing table legs. There would be a moment of frozen silence and then, united by the laser flash of eyes or a single twitch, the wild gallop would be resumed until finally interrupted by the crash of dislodged treasures.

Chapter 8

Troublesome Neighbours

When, later that afternoon, Leonie reached the large white house with Faith and Toga, described by the mysterious woman driver, they agreed that it was the perfect resting place for an itinerant animal. There were stables filled with straw, an almost unrecognisable kitchen garden and beyond, at least an acre of overgrown lawns surrounded by trees and a dense shrubbery concealing a maze of little paths. Now and then, a few chickens could be heard; an ideal sanctuary for a homeless creature. Following Celia Hammond's advice, Leonie put some cat food she had brought with her on the steps of the veranda which overlooked the lawns and would be bathed in the morning with warm autumn sunlight.

They then crossed St Mary's Drive, as Acajou would have done, to a little private road called Faversham Lane. Here they saw four or five cats sunning themselves in porches or on their garden walls. Suddenly, Faith hesitated – sitting on a patch of grass near what was probably his own garden gate, was a brown cat but even from where they were standing Faith could see by the shape of his face and the china blue eyes that he was not Acajou but she agreed that she would hold Toga so that Leonie could approach and stroke him and, just for her own satisfaction, feel his collar.

"Forward about ten paces – now on to the grass, go

carefully, he's there, still sitting —" Toga whimpered and Leonie thought he might run away. She moved quietly and slowly and then she put out her hand. He was wearing a velvet collar, not a leather one. Leonie guessed what must have been going through Faith's mind. The collar was green and she wondered if this was the brown cat that had been seen crossing the road by the woman driver? In spite of the warmth of the sun, a sick chill crept over her but she decided to cling on to the slender thread of hope and they continued walking.

An elderly gentleman, one of the band of genteel leaf sweepers, bade them "Good day!" as they passed and Leonie asked him if he had seen a glossy brown cat? He had not but he volunteered information about some of those they had seen scattered along Faversham Lane in their sundry restful poses. He said he would, however, keep an eye open for Acajou and suggested that they should go to the large white house almost opposite the end of Faversham Lane whose straw filled stables, he thought, would be of interest to any cat.

"Mice and what have you", he chuckled.

On hearing that they had already been there, he continued, "Well now, there's a lady, a splendid character who keeps a few chickens in a makeshift run behind the old kitchen garden, the straw's hers. She visits them three or four times a day and she'd keep a lookout for you, I'm sure."

Faith and Leonie had supposed the clucking sound to come from the neighbouring garden. It was pleasing to think that such a potentially fruitful site would be under regular observation.

"Miss Allerdyce," he said – it was the perfect day for a chat – "is a rather quaint and eccentric soul, a very cultured lady who devotes all her love, energy and her money to the injured and threatened hens and cocks."

In Castleridge, there was a cattle market held each Monday in the car park down by the station. Animals were transported to this site in lorries, often confined in cramped and unpleasant conditions to be sold to the highest bidder; the buyer's money only being sought, not his good intentions.

Emily Allerdyce, it transpired, had occasionally overheard dubious negotiations and the discussed appraisal of a bird's stamina or fighting record rather than its ancestry so, whenever possible, she will buy the cock in question to give it sanctuary in her own home.

"It also upsets her to see the woebegone hens with bedraggled feathers and damaged wings crushed together in unsuitable cages and obviously in distress. These, too, she buys and she has written innumerable letters to the authorities responsible for the organisation of the market as well as to the newspapers but, apparently, no one wants to know."

"How does she manage now?" Leonie asked.

"I'm afraid she has been banned from going to the market altogether now lest she should deter other would-be purchasers by making public her obvious concern for the welfare of the birds. Once rescued," he laughed, "her refugees can cause still more problems. Wilfred, her latest acquisition, has an exceedingly lusty crow and, quite naturally, he likes to practise at dawn which makes him unpopular in a residential area with many commuting neighbours and there have been several complaints. The late Miss Ruskin, to whom the white house used to belong, felt sorry for Miss Allerdyce and when she was no longer permitted to keep her disadvantaged charges in the tiny garden behind her terraced cottage, Miss Ruskin had offered her a small plot of land behind the kitchen garden believing that the screen of trees and the increased distance from the neighbours would prevent any further complaints."

The sight and sound of strutting, clucking and pecking poultry would be exciting for Acajou and if he had entered this wild garden, he would be quite happy to while away the hours watching them through the wire netting and the crowing in the early morning and evening would help him to find the house again if he should wander too far on his continued quest for home.

Despite the fact that she had not met Miss Allerdyce, Leonie felt grateful for the kindness she bestowed on these feathered waifs and she entirely approved of her principles.

When she inquired from whom she could gain permission to investigate the white house grounds more thoroughly, she was sad to learn that the lovely house had been acquired by one of the many anonymous property developers who intended to demolish it and build in its place a block of flats.

"Don't worry about trespassing," the old gentleman had said, "the whole place has gone to seed over the last nine months and I'm sure no one will object to you being in the garden."

They walked on for almost an hour and then decided that a drive along the whole of the egg van route would be a good idea before Faith left. Finally, they reached Montague Crescent and the boys' school upon whose gate Leonie taped another little yellow notice.

Faith had to be home soon so, discussing the pros and cons of local planning decisions and the Green Belt policy with the resultant in-filling, squeezing as many houses as possible into previously lovely gardens which was spoiling their little market town, they drove home and had a quick cup of coffee before Faith left. Leonie was so pleased to have had such a long and satisfactory hunt for Acajou.

It had been a pleasant walk and during the course of their travels, they had talked to one or two delightful people and heard almost complete life histories over the garden walls.

The prospects were improving: the Brownies, the children from the primary school at the bottom of Pine Hill Avenue and now the boys from Castleridge secondary school. Soon there would be hundreds of pairs of bright young eyes looking for Acajou on Leonie's behalf. Gradually, the sense of frustration was beginning to subside but she was becoming convinced by the nagging thought that Acajou's retrieval could only be accomplished with the aid of sight. He would soon discover that in the wild his safety could be jeopardised by calling out with his lusty Burmese "Meow" and she began to fear that he might not make an audible response to her call. If this were so, what chance had she of finding him on her own. She could quite easily walk straight past him but, of course, Toga would not do that without a significant reaction. If only – in the same way that a dog has a vigorous shoulder shake when perplexed or worried, Leonie shrugged hers and returning to contemplation of the real world, she managed to calm the mounting turmoil in her brain; a well-practised art in learning to control her impatience. During this week, she had come to know several neighbours who had shown great kindness. The walk with Faith had given them both pleasure and she never failed to be interested by the diversity of personalities and the multitude of extraordinary facets to be discovered in human nature.

Chapter 9

Reversed Charges

Leonie had not been home from hospital for more than ten minutes when the phone rang.

"Will you take a reversed charge call?" the operator asked.

Who, she mused, would be calling her in Castleridge on a reversed charge?

"Yes, certainly," she replied. Then a child spoke, probably a young boy.

"We've seen a dark brown cat in the shed at the bottom of a garden; it is in Ashfield Road. Have you found yours?"

"How marvellous!" Leonie said, "Thank you so much for ringing me. Do tell me the exact address."

"We were playing in the alley that runs past the end of these gardens and we saw it," he continued, "and there is a huge conker tree near the hedge and he's wearing a green collar."

"I wonder if you could run along to the end of the alley and down Ashfield Road to see if you can see a number on the gate?" Leonie suggested.

"Er – please, er – " he stammered nervously, "what are you going to do about the reward?"

She laughed. "Ring me back in about half an hour and I promise you, if the cat is mine, the reward is yours." She had to think quickly, who could she ask to go with her to Ashfield Road and, as the boy seemed disinclined to find the number, she decided that, with help, she could find the road and then walk down the alleyway until they found the large horse chestnut tree. She wouldn't be able to find it on her own – Lindsay perhaps, she wondered, if she is in?

"And do reverse the charges again," she added, "and thank you so much for looking for the cat and taking the trouble to find a phone box and call me!"

He sounded about ten or eleven years old. She could just picture him – skinny, holes in the knees of his jeans and an eager little face. Leonie was impressed by his resourcefulness in reversing the charges. He probably had no money with him and so much time would have been wasted if he had gone home to find some.

Her pulse racing, she telephoned Lindsay who was at home and, as luck would have it, had just finished painting the skirting board in her kitchen. She agreed to drive her to Ashfield Road as soon as she had washed her hands and it would only take about ten minutes.

Ashfield Road was, indeed, one that Acajou could have reached had he alighted from the egg van at its second stop. By wandering through a few gardens, he could have come to this spot eventually to find shelter and, perhaps, taken up residence in the shed.

She knocked on the door of number 52. It was a smart detached house in a prosperous part of the town, but there was no reply. Diffidently, they made their way around to the back of the house where there were two steps down to the lawn and at the far end of the garden, they saw the huge old horse chestnut tree that they had found when walking down the alley to identify the house. Together, Leonie and Lindsay crossed the grass and looked through a small window in the rickety old shed and there he was – a beautiful brown cat.

"I'm sorry, love, but I don't think he's yours," Lindsay said sadly. "He doesn't seem quite the right colour. He's more a sort of mid-brown and yours was a darker brown, as far as I remember, wasn't he? And has he got a white patch under his chin? Do you want to feel him to be sure?"

She was not really an animal person and had never paid much attention to the cats when visiting Leonie and Andrew for a cup of coffee and she couldn't recall Acajou's exact appearance. Mid-brown? Leonie wasn't sure exactly what colour "mid" might be to Lindsay but she knew that Acajou's coat was a rich dark colour and there was definitely no white patch under his chin. She put out her hand. Her dreams were dashed! He was a tame and trusting cat and purred as he allowed her to fondle him and to examine his collar. It was another velvet one and there was no bell and no disc.

Crazy thoughts jostled for space in Leonie's head: just

suppose he had been stolen as so many friends had feared. A thief would have changed the collar immediately. The theft of cats had been in the headlines of late and there had been grotesque pictures in the papers and on the television of cat pelts hanging in rows like lines of washing to be sold and made up into fur coats. Certain colours were reputed to be in great demand for the export market and the thieves were specialising in the collection of these. The skinned bodies of several cats had been discovered dumped in a pond near Maidstone. Hastily, she brushed the thoughts away and decided that the thieves would have a hard time trying to find pelts to match Acajou's. This cat wasn't quite large enough nor had he mewed as Acajou would have done as she had approached him. He was also calm and unafraid, obviously accustomed to this environment. His owner probably went out to work by day and lavished affection on him in the evening.

Poor Lindsay was embarrassed and appeared to feel sorry that she could not produce for her the right cat. Leonie took from her pocket some of the tiny Munchies she had brought with her and he crunched them with relish.

When Danny phoned again, he introduced himself this time, he was buoyant with anticipation and Leonie longed to tell him that he had won his prize but she could only express her gratitude for all that he had done and point out how clever he had been to find a brown Burmese cat but unfortunately, not hers. Danny was naturally disappointed but she resolved to reward him for his effort and give him a small token of thanks. However, before she could ask him where he lived, he said goodbye in a sad little voice and put down the receiver.

Dear Lindsay offered to go walking with her later in the afternoon and so, at four o'clock, they set off once more to search, call and listen until it was dark. They posted notices

Reversed Charges

through letter boxes and attached some to more trees and fences and Leonie derived some comfort from the fact that the news of Acajou's disappearance was being spread in a way that she could not have achieved by herself. Lindsay was an entertaining and cheery companion and made light of the fact that she must have wasted hours of her precious time, insisting that she needed the exercise and the walk was just what she had fancied.

"Couldn't waste this fantastic weather, could we?"

When Andrew came home that evening, checking on his way which houses had been reoccupied, they set off once more after dinner following the route of the egg van and calling in at the white house on the way to leave some more cat food. The meat that Leonie had left in the morning had gone but she knew full well that it could have been consumed by any one of a hundred creatures. The possibility that Acajou was using the white house as a home base was not totally without complication. A little further up the road, there was a small group of semi-detached houses, one of which was inhabited by an eccentric art teacher from Hollybourne School who kept hoards of cats, as many as fifty at one time, or so it was rumoured. As none of them was allowed outside in the garden, the logistics of the situation boggled the mind. Crispin, Acajou and Paprika's eldest son, who had been given to one of Prudence's young school friends, Alison, disappeared in this area a couple of years ago under rather mysterious circumstances.

Large boxes of liver or fish often stood in the art teacher's porch, presumably delivered to her in order to feed her cats but they seemed to have a magnetic effect on others in the district.

Alison had a gnawing suspicion that Crispin had been attracted by the liver and had possibly been mistakenly thought to be a stray and had been invited in to join the rest.

Seeing is Deceiving

She had attempted to make contact with Miss Argelle but neither the doorbell nor the telephone were ever answered. When Alison contacted the RSPCA, they spoke of Miss Argelle in glowing terms as incredibly caring, saving the lives of countless cats. Alison was advised to write a letter to this solitary lady to see if Crispin's description coincided with any in the "Rescue Haven" but this, too, remained unanswered. Alison also learned from a neighbour's child, who attended the same school as the art teacher, that the cats were frequently used as models, sitting quietly in their cages waiting to be drawn or painted and one, she felt sure, was a Burmese cat.

Day after day, on her way home from school, Alison would look up at Miss Argelle's bedroom windows to see if she could recognise Crispin's face among the six or seven cats who gazed down at her from the window sills but she never saw him again and still wondered sometimes if he was living in one of the rooms at the back of the house.

Leonie mentioned her concerns to Mrs Wagoner, a lady whose telephone number she had been given by the RSPCA, a cat lover and certain to be a willing helper in the retrieval of Acajou if at any time he should be seen. Mrs Wagoner had a slightly clipped but polished accent, English not being her native tongue, and she began to tell her all about Miss Argelle, a most unusual person and obsessed with cats, seeming to have acquired many highly bred strays.

"While I was weeding a flower bed in my front garden one afternoon," she told Leonie, "I looked up to see Miss Argelle with whom I was previously on nodding terms only. She was passing my garden on her way to the shops, staring into my kitchen window. I turned and saw that she was looking at Samuel, my British Blue, who could be seen quite clearly curled up on a cushion on a high stool in the sunny corner. She seemed to be talking to herself.

'Beauuutiful, exquisite, enchanting!' she was murmuring, almost cooing. I put down my trowel and we chatted for a bit and she told me all about her marvellous collection of cats, adding wistfully that she had never owned a British Blue! It was a lovely day and weeds can always wait so I invited her in for a cup of tea so that she could be introduced properly to Samuel and admire him at close quarters. He has a very good pedigree – "but am I keeping you?" she suddenly asked.

"Goodness, no!" Leonie replied, "I am enthralled. Do please carry on."

"Well," she continued, "she accepted my invitation with surprising alacrity, so, leaving my half-filled trug on the lawn, we went inside. While I was changing my shoes in the kitchen, we went in through the backdoor. Miss Argelle walked straight on through to the sitting room. I switched on the kettle quickly and set out two cups and saucers and biscuits on a tray, then followed her in, reminding myself one ought to be just a little careful about strangers but all was well. Sammy, always keen to be stroked, had gone ahead and Miss Argelle who was sitting beside him on the sofa, was almost in a trance. She seemed to purr with delight herself as she caressed him and described a feeling of 'oneness' as she touched his soft fur.

Then, seeming to return from her enchanted state, she murmured something about a British Blue. Blue, in the cat world, you understand, is a euphemism for grey and although Sammy is a splendid grey cat, I was a little disconcerted by the effect he had on her."

Leonie smiled audibly and encouraged her to continue.

"Well, we conversed over tea and," she confided, "I became more and more curious. Do you know, I would have loved Miss Argelle to have invited me back to her home to meet her family of cats. I can't think how she copes with so many, can you? How on earth do you think she organises the hygiene? Anyway, she stayed on for about half an hour and she told me that she was giving up her hobby of collecting stray cats saying that, from now on, she was going to concentrate all her energy on the support of a child in India. We discussed the scheme and both agreed that it was a worthwhile charity and deserved her obvious wish to do something that could involve both her practical and mental abilities. Miss Argelle said she intended to write weekly letters and study the chosen child's language so that she could communicate 'soul to soul'. She said that she was about to resign from her post as an art teacher at the local girls' school and was now going to devote herself to an entirely new field of study. Then," she continued, "she began to tell me in a confidential tone how she had become completely engrossed in the progress and the education of her Indian child and all things Indian. She then fished into the deep recesses of her large handbag and withdrew a piece of parchment-like paper covered in the most beautiful hand-written but illegible script. She handed it to me and then waited in silence. I said that it was absolutely fascinating but I couldn't read it and asked her what it said. She looked pained and sighed before whispering in a quiet little voice, 'How disappointing! I thought you might just be the person to help me and that I had been led here this afternoon by a higher being. You see,' she explained, 'I am in communication with a spirit from the other side. This writing is mine and I was instructed to do it by the spirit but I cannot read it. What a pity you are not willing to help me.'

"I protested that of course I would have done so had I been able and suggested that perhaps she could take it to a school for oriental languages where she would surely be able to find someone to give her a translation and then, do you know, she stood up, thanked me for the cup of tea and left without another word."

Leonie murmured that it was indeed extraordinary but Mrs Wagoner had yet more to tell.

"That's not all," she persisted. "A couple of weeks later, I met her in the supermarket and as I was paying my bill, she leant forward and putting her lips to my ear, she whispered: 'Now I am the proud owner, too, of a truly noble British Blue!' and she told me how she had seen it in Yardley Road, not far from the vet's. 'Quite obviously a stray,' she assured me, 'because he was still in the garden the following day when I returned with my special cage.'

"You can imagine what I was thinking by this time and then she said that she caught it quite easily and she boasted that she was a most skilful cat catcher. The girl at the till gave me my change and when I turned round, Miss Argelle had vanished!"

Leonie was horrified! She did not like the thought of a cage and she suggested that the cat probably lived in the house to which the garden belonged. Highly bred cats like that would be kept indoors at night and permitted to wander afield by day.

Mrs Wagoner agreed but said that she had not seen Miss Argelle since then but suggested it might be worth Leonie trying to phone her and see if she had caught sight of Acajou anywhere. She did say that she was giving up the hobby of stray gathering apart from that British Blue, so she might be willing to help.

Leonie had already decided not to communicate with Miss Argelle as she would find her adorable Acajou quite irresistible and he would probably make the perfect companion for her recently acquired British Blue. Mrs Wagoner sounded educated and a sensible woman, not given to hyperbole or distortion of the truth. The story was, indeed, an extraordinary one. Finally, she said that if Leonie had any news of Acajou, she would be delighted to offer her services and drive her wherever necessary.

"By the way," she added, "I think we have met. "My thirteen-year-old daughter, Helena, goes to Abbeyfield Hall and I think I have seen you there on parents' evenings or at concerts. Am I right in thinking you have a black labrador?"

"You are indeed!" Leonie replied and they chatted about school and dogs for a while. She told Leonie about the two poodles and the West-Highland terrier that she had once owned, "and I doted on them, of course" she said. "I think they were very clever little dogs but I never fail to marvel at Toga's ability when I watch her at work with you."

Then and there, Leonie decided that if Andrew or Lindsay were to be unavailable, Mrs Wagoner would be just the right person to ask for assistance should there be any news of Acajou.

Chapter 10

Picnic at Dawn

It was 3 a.m. and Leonie was wearying of the "Through the Night" programme on LBC which consisted of inconsequential phone calls to an argumentative presenter when the idea suddenly came to her. The last three callers had been debating the relative importance of the type of food chosen for picnics; one waxing lyrical over prawn and avocado vol-au-vents accompanied by foil wrapped asparagus tips and another protesting that Marmite or cheese sandwiches with lettuce and a bit of salad dressing were far more filling and the kids loved them.

At dawn, the time of day recommended by Celia Hammond for serious searching, Leonie would assemble the picnic gear: a small camping stove, fuelled by a canister of butane gas, matches, (those would be harder to find as they were only required for picnics or birthday candles), a saucepan, a bottle of water and a piece of frozen fish. Andrew was not at all keen on the idea when she mentioned it to him in the morning but, sensing her determination, he agreed to help so, at seven o'clock, they set off with Toga to the White Lodge.

Andrew felt distinctly ill at ease trespassing on another's property but Leonie's arguments were persuasive.

The garden was indeed a wilderness. An enormous oak tree sprawled across the lawn where it must have lain undisturbed since the legendary gales in October 1987.

Picnic at Dawn

Pieces of guttering and shattered slate were strewn on the patio outside the French windows. They walked down one of the narrow paths almost completely obscured by weeds. It curved gently between rose beds and into the shrubbery beyond the lawn where they discovered an enchanting little summerhouse. This was the ideal spot in which to set up the enticement device for there was great potential as a port in a storm. Leonie lit the stove and poured some water from the bottle on to the fish already in the pan. The fish was still frozen and it seemed an eternity before the water boiled but, when eventually it did, she wafted the emanating steam with her hands to scatter the tempting vapours to the four winds, none of which were in evidence on that mild October Saturday morning. While she wafted, Andrew further explored the garden. Every movement in the grass or rustle of leaves brought fleeting moments of hope but again, they drew a blank. Andrew did concede, however, that this was a congenial environment. Having tossed the fish on to the grass, she emptied the water from the pan, splattering it as far afield as possible in order to increase the catchment area for a cat in pursuit of a fishy trail, reminding herself of Hansel and Gretel with their bread crumbs in the forest. Momentarily, her melancholic mood evaporated and she laughed aloud. How her son, Thomas, would chide her: first of all, Madame Poirot or Juliet Bravo following minuscule clues and now, Mrs H. Anderson, rewriting her own fairy tales. Leonie was a romantic at heart and, when in her teens, she had read a book called *The Prisoner of Zenda* about Rupert of Henzau and decided that when the time came, she would definitely marry a noble knight or a prince. Her dream virtually came true but her prince did not actually wear a crown and he did not dance very well but he was wise, intelligent, patient and loving. She had enjoyed dancing and had even won a national ballroom dancing competition just before she qualified as a physiotherapist. The fact that partners held hands for most of the time in ballroom dancing meant that blindness was no disadvantage. Andrew was good looking, approximately ten inches taller than Leonie, slim with fairish hair and piercing blue eyes. Leonie's were blue too as were those of all three of their children. Impatiently, Toga gave a noisy shake so that even her ears flapped and she was rewarded with a flake of coley and they made their way out of the garden and back up the hill towards home.

After breakfast, they drove along the road in which Murphy's Free Range Eggs had been delivered, posting and sticking up more notices but, as this was the first time Andrew had done the journey in the daylight, they were able to search more thoroughly and spend longer in the more promising locations. During the afternoon, there was a phone call which Andrew answered from a woman who said that her husband was out in the garden digging up a dahlia tuber and had just been in to tell her that he had been approached and had his legs rubbed by a Siamese type of cat with a "stripy tail." Andrew laughed and responded rather too jovially, Leonie thought.

"Lucky fellow, but I'm afraid he doesn't sound like ours. He is Burmese, not Siamese, nor does he sport a stripy tail but thank you very much for calling, – Goodbye," – and, rather too abruptly it seemed, he replaced the receiver. Leonie had wanted to talk to this person, to anyone who had seen any cat that might vaguely resemble theirs. Andrew hadn't asked enough questions and most people were unable to distinguish one breed from another. Inside, she was quite unreasonably exasperated but Andrew maintained that no one could mistake Acajou's indisputably monochromatic, mahogany brown tail for a stripy one. Leonie declined his offer to go shopping with her to buy the weekly food, explaining that she did not wish to miss any telephone calls at that time of day.

On Sunday morning, Leonie repeated the fish cooking ritual before going to church and looked forward to seeing their elder daughter who had phoned before breakfast to say that she would be coming home for lunch and to help with the search. Olivia always had an electrifying effect on the household and the pace of everything was quickened from the moment she arrived.

Lunch having been prepared at breakneck speed, Leonie and Olivia were able to go out in the car together leaving it to cook and Andrew to get on with his paper work while they took a handful of notices to every school in the locality. As they drove along the High Street, Olivia hopped out at almost every lamppost, adhering the little yellow strips of paper and, seeing a police woman watching her from a shop doorway where she was standing with her walkie-talkie, she asked her if they were contravening any laws. Headquarters was contacted and the reply came that bill sticking was nothing to do with the police: it was the council that might object. A few showers would unglue them and all would be well, Leonie decided, before the council ever got to hear of it.

After lunch, they took Toga to the park where Olivia could continue to look for Acajou while simultaneously being refreshed after a busy week in London by the glorious autumn colours in the Kent countryside. Soon after tea, she left again by train as her parents did not like her to travel in the dark nor were they happy about her safety in the underground system late at night. Everything was suddenly very flat.

On Monday afternoon, reluctantly Leonie went to Craybridge for her sewing class hating to leave the telephone unattended and longing for the day when the answer-phone would be installed and she could know that not one single chance had been missed. On the way home, the trains were delayed and it was past five o'clock before she was able to feed the animals. No sooner had Toga commenced the happy crunching when the phone rang. The voice was that of a lady, probably in the latter part of her middle years, saying that she had tried to contact her earlier in the afternoon.

"I think I've seen your cat," she began, "I presume you haven't found him yet?"

"No, no, do tell me more!" Leonie urged.

"Well, my dear, he was dark brown and glossy with a green collar which looked like leather and he was crossing the road, St Mary's Drive, that is, I live a little way down on the left, and I was in the front garden pulling up a few weeds when he came and stood quite still just watching me. He was only about six feet away, I could have touched him but I didn't know what to do and I didn't know his name so I couldn't call him. If he comes again, do you want me to try and catch him and keep him in the house for you?"

"Yes please," she said, "do try and take him in and I will come and collect him immediately."

"Well," she continued, "I hurried indoors to try and telephone you but you weren't there." (Leonie was overwhelmed with regret.)

"And, when I went into the garden again, I saw him disappearing in the direction of the Methodist church. The garden there, you know, is rather overgrown and I would imagine an ideal place for cats. The thing is," she persisted, "I'm not very used to cats and I don't know how to handle them."

Leonie did not want her to scare him away with her efforts to catch him so she suggested that, if she had a car, she could open the door and he would almost certainly hop inside.

"That's a good idea," the caller agreed, "then I wouldn't have to frighten him by picking him up. He probably doesn't like strangers anyway. We often leave our car out in the driveway during the day."

Leonie was overjoyed and thanked her for her concern and for taking the trouble to ring a second time.

"And by the way," she added, "you mustn't worry about him, my dear, he looks sleek and shiny and in the peak of condition!"

"How marvellous!" Leonie exclaimed and thanked her again for being the harbinger of such wonderful news. She gave her name, Eveline Harris, and her address and asked to be told if anyone found him.

A rush of adrenaline made Leonie's heart feel like a caged bird beating its wings against her ribs and she astonished Toga by breaking into song as she hurried to the kitchen to take her lead and harness down from the hook behind the door. With trembling fingers and explaining the plan aloud to Toga, she fastened the lead to her collar and clipped the strap of the harness around her chest, being careful not to trap any fur in the buckle before collecting a piece of Sunday's chicken from the fridge and wrapping it in kitchen paper. She brushed her hair, threw on a jacket and together, they left the house at full trot.

As they crossed the two roads at the top of the hill taking a short cut past the ornamental pond in the Memorial Garden, Leonie reflected on the fact as she reached St Mary's Drive that nothing could have intimated to Acajou, if he was lost in this area, that familiar territory would lie beyond this point. Only in flight over the old police station could a crow have told him how close he was to home. Walking up and down St Mary's Drive, she called and listened. She was not sure of the exact location of the Methodist church, nor did she feel too happy about exploring the land behind it in the dark. Seeing her hesitation, a kind passer-by crossed the road to ask if she needed help and gratefully, Leonie accepted. After explaining the situation, she asked if she could be directed to the church. The instructions were clear: it was on the left, just a few yards from the main road and the minister's house was almost directly opposite.

"Would you like me to take you there?" he offered, "and we'll see what he says."

The minister had only that afternoon returned from a holiday and had seen no unusual cats about but he agreed to take Leonie across the road to look. Having picked up a torch from the hall table, he took her hand and she and Toga followed him in single file as they threaded their

Picnic at Dawn

way between the church and an overgrown hedge, under overhanging bushes and down a narrow path that led to the back of the building where there was a dustbin, a small shed and a wild garden.

"A splendid spot for a refugee," he murmured, "and all these leaves must conceal innumerable juicy morsels for a predator." He also mentioned the existence of another untended garden belonging to a derelict house further down St. Mary's Drive and he promised to keep an eye open for him. As they retraced their steps, he apologised that they had had no luck and then considerately inquired, "Know where you are, now that we're back on the pavement?"

Thanking him for all his help she said she did and, shaking her firmly by the hand, he bade her farewell.

How far could Acajou have wandered in these last few hours, she wondered? When Andrew came home, he had a far more positive attitude. Straight after dinner they set off together and having deposited food at the usual sites, they took some to place on the ground near the church dustbin. It seemed quite possible that Acajou could have jumped out of the van at its first port of call, having been frightened by the noisy engine and a lurching journey.

They knocked on the door of number seven and were invited in by Mrs Harris, the afternoon caller. Both she and her husband described Acajou to perfection noting even the way in which his collar seemed to stand away from his neck. They were quite right; the collar was brand new and still rather stiff. Mr Harris then punctured Leonie's optimism with an arrow of doubt.

"Did you know that a family a little further down this road have a couple of Burmese cats but this is the first time we think we have seen this one?"

The family, they discovered, had a daughter who had been at school with Olivia and they attended St. Nicholas

Church too. Leonie decided that she would follow Celia Hammond's advice and ring them to ask for a detailed description of their cats and the colour of their collars.

Mrs Greaves was sympathetic and she described with some pride her lilac and chocolate Burmese cats, respectively Crocus and Crumb. The latter, she said, was a very light brown and, although his collar was green, it was velvet and grubby and fitted snuggly to his neck. Leonie thanked her for her help and once again, her spirits rose to a peek in those continuing undulations of hope and despair. The safety net was tightening around Acajou and with Mrs Harris's description of his state of well-being along with her general optimism, hers was restored.

Leonie could hardly sleep that night and at six o'clock in the morning, Tuesday, the 1st of November, she crept downstairs, harnessed Toga and set off for the Methodist church. She knew that she would be able to hear the slightest sound in the stillness of the early morning before the birds woke and before the roads were filled with the unceasing drone of traffic and the pavements with commuters dashing to the station. Tuesday was a bad day for tracing Acajou, as the morning was taken up with work at the hospital and the afternoon with her computer lesson. Roll on Friday, she thought when all the phone messages would at last be recorded and stored in the new answerphone.

Andrew and Leonie continued with the food distribution at dawn and at dusk on the Wednesday morning, they noticed that the gate of the now defunct nursery was open and there were cars in the driveway. The shop, in which the produce had been sold, was on the Dyneford Road fifty or so yards beyond St Mary's Drive and its land extended behind the end of the gardens in that road. Although they suspected that Acajou had been spending some time in this area, they had not considered until that day when doing their rounds a little later than usual, that he could have wandered into the nursery. It looked very promising. There were a few upturned wooden crates by the gravel path, dilapidated potting sheds and greenhouses with broken windows. As there were fragments of glass on the path, Leonie and Toga waited while Andrew did a more thorough investigation. She looked at her watch; it was time he was leaving to catch his train.

She heard footsteps on the gravel. "This looks jolly hopeful," Andrew said, "and believe it or not, in one of the sheds, curled up on a tatty old cushion there was a large black and white cat fast asleep. There's no doubt about it, we must come again but now I must dash, my train is due in twelve minutes. We must start leaving sustenance here too for Acajou and any cronies."

Lindsay phoned at lunch time to see if there was any news and if Leonie would like to go trekking with her again.

"A marvellous afternoon for a walk," she enthused, not a bit like the 2nd of November."

"Not a lot," Leonie replied, "but the gates of the old nursery were open and Andrew thought it looked a possible site and one to search more thoroughly. He saw a black and white cat sleeping in one of the old sheds. I would like to leave some food there too.", she added.

"Well now," Lindsay exclaimed, "there's a stroke of luck. The house next door to Crester's Nursery has been taken over by the Missionary Society and John Billing – do you know him from church – well, I'm sure he would be only too pleased to let us go and have a look around the garden."

It was a beautiful garden, secluded and peaceful,

shielded from the Dyneford Road by the house and well established trees. Part of the fence ran alongside some of the nursery outbuildings. A tortoiseshell cat was sunning itself beneath a rhododendron at the far end of the garden and, as they crossed the lawn to stroke it, a black and white one slipped through the fence and into the nursery but there was no sign of Acajou. Leonie then suggested that they might visit the derelict house in St Mary's Drive.

Lindsay and Leonie were hesitant about exploring this venue too thoroughly, not having gained permission to do so, but they did hear a clucking of hens beyond the stables. They could not see them, even though they walked through a small yard and past the stables out on to a gravel path that led to a rickety gate. This opened on to a narrow lane which led them back to the main road and they decided to go home having had a good hour out in some very interesting spots and Leonie was rather keen to be within reach of the phone once again.

Leonie did so wish she could have touched those cats in the Missionary Society garden. Blindness was a real inconvenience sometimes! She could picture those "well established" trees and the sleeping cat on the lawn but only just; even a detailed description was only partially satisfying. She had found compensations however, from time to time.

Leonie could imagine that fallen oak on the White Lodge lawn. In their own garden, acorns seeded themselves as well as hazelnuts and they had grown into small trees along with a beech tree and holly bushes which Andrew had dug up for her. Together, they had planted them in large pots so that she could watch them grow, so to speak, and examine carefully with her hands the detail of the leaves and the general outline and shape of an oak tree, for example, in a miniature version. One of the acorns had

Picnic at Dawn

taken root at the foot of the steps to the upper lawn and so she had planted a small oak on the other side of the steps and coaxed them both into a gentle curve as they grew, clipping off any little unwanted branches, so that, after a few years, they eventually became handrails. She secured the leafy crowns with pieces of rope to the two supports of the rose arch at the top of the steps.

Leonie had always fancied a little woodland of her own. She used to collect leaves, cones or even flowers and decorative grasses to ornament her ceramic creations instead of trying to draw. A leaf pressed lightly into moist porcelain or a cone stroked gently around the sides of an ordinary white clay bowl could produce a delicate design and each season brought new ideas. However, this afternoon Leonie indulged herself without hindrance of any kind by running her fingers over the elegant and silky forms of Suchard and Paprika who came to greet her on her return, cuddling Toga at the same time with one elbow while trying to maintain her balance during the wild welcome. Toga did not appreciate being left at home with just cats for company.

Chapter 11

Introducing Terry and Nige

On the fifth floor of an office in Bromley, a board meeting was in progress. Item Six on the agenda was the proposed demolition of a house, a shop and several out-buildings at number 236, Dyneford Road, Castleridge, Kent. The site, presently known as Crester's Nursery, was due to be prepared for development: a block of flats. A youngish man, with a pinstriped suit and a suppressed Bromley accent, said that he would be able to hire a bulldozer for Saturday, the 19th of November, and that he could arrange for a demolition gang to start work as soon as the machines were in situ. There was a grunt of approval and the motion was passed.

Item Seven on the agenda...

Thursday afternoon and the *Castleridge Chronicle* was spread-eagled on laps and coffee tables throughout the town and there it was: Leonie's plea in the Lost and Found column, waiting to be read.

"Oh Acajou, where are you?" she said aloud, mechanically ascending the stairs to gather yet more laundry to put in the washer. Desperation seemed to clutch at her throat and that old, half-smothered serpent of self-pity writhed inside, rearing its ugly head again. If only she could see, she could hunt so much more effectively than anyone else. Acajou had been missing now for two weeks and she had been haunted by the thought of his inevitable feeling of bewilderment; confusion compounded by nurtured dependence. She began to whisper a prayer: "Please God, help me to find my lost cat!"

A sock fell from the cumbersome bundle of clothes in her arms, but she stood still and continued: "If you are really there, God, please prove it to me this last time and I shall be a faithful and obedient Christian for always."

The telephone rang and Leonie dropped another sock. It was a woman with a young, cheerful voice enquiring if she had yet found the missing cat.

Surely God was not at work already? She felt exhilarated. Was he nudging this young person to make contact and spur her on when dark clouds were gathering or was this merely a coincidence?

"My nine-year-old daughter, Clare, saw a notice on the school gate," she said, "and I see there is also one on the lamppost outside our house. Now, on Tuesday morning and again yesterday, I did see a dark brown cat. I don't know what a Burmese cat looks like but it was an unusual breed and," she laughed, "Clare is adamant that it was Burmese. It came across our back lawn and, a couple of minutes later, I saw it climbing the cherry tree in the front garden of the old Georgian house on the corner. I suppose it must have been about half past seven; the children were having breakfast."

Leonie was delighted and thanked her for giving her such hopeful news and asked where she lived so that she could come with Andrew and look around her area, and, if successful, deliver the reward. It was almost thirty-four hours now since he had been seen but it seemed to be positive proof that Acajou was still alive and wandering within reasonable proximity of St Mary's Drive where he had been spotted on Monday by Mrs Harris. Although the territorial rights of the Burmese cats living close to

Introducing Terry and Nige

her probably included the Georgian house and possibly the nearby wilderness garden, the fact that a brown cat's presence had been noted indicated that it was not one of the local inhabitants.

A torch-lit investigation of the area in the evening with Andrew revealed nothing, but food was placed beneath the hedges there as well as in all the normal sites. As they stood on the veranda of the forlorn house in the wilderness garden, Andrew noticed that the lights beyond the shrubbery were from one of the houses they had just visited and remarked that it was most encouraging to know that Acajou's odyssey seemed to be within a small and fairly well-defined area.

In the morning, along with the first refreshing sip of Earl Grey tea, Leonie savoured a new mood of anticipation. It was Friday, the 4th of November and the eagerly awaited day for the installation of the new answerphone. She caught the bus back from hospital with Toga in order to be home by one o'clock. It only took an hour and a half for Mr Wolf and Eddie to disconnect the old set in the hall and their bedroom and to lay and connect new wires before bringing a ladder from the van to enable Eddie to extricate the old garden extension bell from the clinging tentacles of the clematis above the French windows in the dining-room. It was not clear why this bell needed replacing but Mr Wolf assured Leonie that it did. The answerphone was connected to the new plug in the bedroom and the system was tested.

Leonie asked if it would be possible for one of them to be kind enough to read to her the most important instructions so that she could use the phone immediately. Eddie, the younger of the two men, who had done most of the running up and down the stairs, seemed to be rather confused by the request. He was perfectly competent at his job and gave one the impression of being quite a lad; probably the owner of a Harley Davidson motorbike and almost certainly of an extravagantly modern and brightly coloured hairstyle. Leonie was bemused by his embarrassment. Perhaps he was unable to read? Mr Wolf was almost as reticent but offered to "have a go." Putting his tool bag down by the front door, he said that if she would like to go first, he would follow her up to the bedroom. Lifting the receiver off its cradle, he prodded and poked at a few of the buttons and switches and tried to explain which did what. Then, with horny but well-meaning fingers he seized one of Leonie's and dabbed it here and there on the telephone saying:

"Whatever you do, don't touch this or that one until hubby comes home and has had a chance to study the instructions."

He suggested that she should have a trial run while he watched. She ran her fingers over the number buttons, counted carefully and made a call to her sister. All seemed to be well. She thanked him for his kindness and they went downstairs. He called Eddie who had gone through to the kitchen and was stroking the cats. The two men gathered up their tools and departed.

As the van drew away, there was a faint trilling from upstairs. Leonie sped aloft. It was the new phone but the bell was barely audible. Her sister wanted a brief chat and to check that she was happy with everything. Leonie told her about the bell and she offered to test it by calling once more. Nothing happened and, after five minutes, Leonie phoned her again. The outgoing line seemed to be functioning normally. Elizabeth explained that she had tried to ring her but without success. Leonie panicked. What could she do? The frustration of being completely incommunicado temporarily overwhelmed her. Elizabeth said she would contact British Telecom and acquaint them

Introducing Terry and Nige

with the situation.

When British Telecom phoned a few minutes later, a pleasant woman asked her if Monday morning would be convenient? Her throat was gripped by a tightening sensation but Leonie took a deep breath and explained the reason for the installation of the new answerphone. The woman was very understanding and she said she would see what she could do. Leonie waited – after what seemed like several minutes but was probably only one or two, she spoke again: "We're in luck!" she said. "It just so happens that one of our engineers is in your area later this afternoon and he says he'll pop in as soon as he can."

At twenty past four, the door-bell rang. It was an angel in disguise, the engineer from British Telecom. He remembered coming to their house in the summer to repair one of the old phones. He was a friendly and talkative man. He studied the new appliance and the book of instructions for about five minutes. He turned the instrument upside down, reset all the switches underneath it and then announced triumphantly that he thought he had solved the problem.

"While demonstrating how it worked, Keith Wolf must have knocked this one by accident," he said, and he showed Leonie the offending switch.

"There are three positions for this one," he explained. "The first makes the phone ring quietly. The second and there's no sound at all and the third, where I'm putting it now, causes the bell to ring loudly so that you will be able to hear it downstairs."

Leonie felt a little ashamed; some of the fault must have been hers. Keith had left it on the quiet position but she must have moved it to "Silent" when she had dashed to answer Elizabeth's call.

Saturday morning was devoted to the interpretation of innumerable instructions and compliance with them revealed a major fault. The memory buttons, which were supposed to simplify the attainment of routinely required phone numbers, refused to function. How tedious! They would have to go to Tunbridge Wells after all to exchange it and waste most of the afternoon.

There was just sufficient time at the onset of twilight to do a complete tour of all the locations in which Acajou had been seen and to refurbish the food supply. Leonie felt oppressed by a sense of urgency, for it was the 5th of November and there would be fireworks and bonfires: a night of terror for most animals and especially the homeless.

Chapter 12

Forsaken

It was now the 5th of November and sixteen days since Acajou had eaten a proper meal from his own small dish and he was aware of an aching hunger. He was still glossy and fit but rather lean. Keeping close to the fence or well tucked under the hedge, he made his way through two or three gardens, past the nursery and across the road to the Methodist Church. It had previously proved to be a fairly productive area in which to scavenge and one day he had even found a small piece of coley near the dustbin. He had always enjoyed coley but never before had it tasted quite so good. In the region of the dustbin, he had frequently found scraps to eat but other cats tended to travel the same circuit. Sometimes there were small pieces of meat or a fish's head, a diet to which he had become accustomed in his formative years. His fellow travellers must have been astonished to find such catty delicacies, just ready for the taking but it was Acajou's turn tonight. His nose quivered. His inspection of the debris by the dustbin rewarded him with something that smelt scrumptious wrapped in a paper handkerchief. It was chicken. Greedily, he gobbled the juicy morsel and walked on, directing his steps toward the wild garden; a wilderness in which he had recently caught a mouse for supper.

Eyes glowing, sinews taut, in the shelter of the beech hedge he waited. What was that? A light went on in the

Seeing is Deceiving

house but he was not really afraid. More lights and loud music began to blare through the broken windows. Then, there were footsteps, more and still more – laughter and people shouting. The garden was filled with the sound of partygoers. Acajou decided that it was impossible to hunt under these conditions so he turned to go back the way he had come. There was a crash and the sound of breaking glass. Then, there was still more shouting and screaming and running feet. An enormous bang shook the night followed by another and yet another. The sky, already pin pointed with stars, was suddenly lit with streaks of fire which burst into cascades of iridescent sparks and the rocket debris seemed to rain down around him as, crazed with fear, he fled unseeing straight across the road. Brakes screeched ...

Strong hands lifted him gently and laid his limp body on the pavement beside the low wall.

Chapter 13

The Feathered Refugees

At half past eight on Sunday morning, as Andrew and Leonie were eating breakfast, the new telephone trilled in the hall. With a little manoeuvring of the furniture in order to accommodate the transformer within reach of a mains plug, they had brought it downstairs for greater convenience. It was a man who spoke and asked if they had yet found the lost cat?

"Only I don't really know the difference between a Siamese and a Burmese cat and I've just seen something like that on the fire escape. I work here at the Hoe and Sickle hotel down by the station and I read one of your notices on the lamppost at the corner. He was here yesterday afternoon and I think he's here again under the hedge near our car park in the front."

Leonie thanked him and said they would come straight away. Andrew swallowed the last mouthful of his kipper and hurried upstairs to shower. Elated, Leonie dressed quickly and, while he shaved, she wrapped up a few flakes of kipper from her plate. Here at last was a sighting when Andrew was available to take action with her. She called Toga, who had already been fed and picked up her lead, ready to drive down to the station.

They parked the car a little way along the road and walked quietly towards the hotel. There was a movement in the dense foliage behind the wall of the neighbouring house. Leonie called softly and unwrapped the fish. Toga pressed her nose expectantly into her hand so she offered her a flake and shortened the lead to prevent her from overwhelming Acajou with her exuberant greeting – but the precaution, sadly, was unnecessary.

The main door of the hotel was open. As they entered, a man came forward to meet them.

"Ah," he said, "do come in. Are you the people I phoned about the cat?" And he invited them to follow him through to the kitchen and into the garden at the back where he pointed out the fire-escape. There were two dustbins and he suggested that it was probably the waste food they contained that had attracted the cat. Andrew looked under the hedges and peered among the bushes that separated the hotel grounds from the private house next door, but in vain. Leonie thanked the hotel manager for his endeavours and left with him a tin of cat food which was kept in the car for such purposes. He agreed to put some out if the cat should return and promised to lure him into a place of safe keeping. They then walked up and down a few roads in the immediate vicinity doing the daily food round before returning to the car in order to drive home again.

On the lunchtime news on the local Kent radio, Leonie was amazed to hear an item about Castleridge. Other members of the police had been called to help the local constabulary to break up an unauthorised house party. More than two hundred youngsters had assembled in a derelict house where there was evidence of tampering with an electricity meter in order to set up hi-fi equipment and disco lights. Several partygoers had been arrested for possession of drugs or for obstructing and abusing the police. It was most unusual to hear Castleridge mentioned in the news but they were not to know that Acajou had been present.

The Feathered Refugees

Andrew had to mark exam papers that afternoon and, as he had spent so much time with Leonie during the last fortnight helping her to look for Acajou, he needed to catch up with his work. Having checked on Suchard and Paprika, who were curled up in a favourite armchair bathed in sunshine, Leonie sent Toga into the garden to relieve herself so that she could go out with her again and visit the various haunts on the cat walk.

The sundry clues to her orientation in an area with which she was not well acquainted were becoming more familiar. Leonie had to rely on information gleaned from ground gradient and texture plus the type of hedge, fence, wall or gate rather than hints garnered from kerb height, traffic flow or a shop smell, all of which were so helpful in the High Street.

Toga fortified herself for the expedition as they descended the steps from the back door by deftly procuring one of the many crab apples that bejewelled the path down to the gate at that time of year.

Autumn was becoming well established. There was a pungent smell of fallen and decaying leaves and now and then her feet skated on hidden acorns as she followed the track which led to the cottages. The whole area was very quiet this afternoon and, on reflection, Leonie realised that, for the last two or three days, she had not heard the hens who tended to gossip gently when they were disturbed by the sound of footsteps. The hen collector – had she seen Acajou, she wondered? Someone had been to the White Lodge stables recently, for a stone had been put on the foil tray on which she had left some titbits; probably to prevent it from being blown away when it was windy. Leonie remembered that her friend, Faith, knew the owner as Miss Allerdyce had taught maths for a while in the junior school where she too, was a teacher. Clearly,

Seeing is Deceiving

Miss Allerdyce was a thoughtful person and it occurred to Leonie that she might be willing to replenish the tray if she were to give her a good supply of cat food. It would certainly reduce the early morning pressure on Andrew and ease his train catching now that they were delivering sustenance to an increasing number of sites.

Leonie decided to phone Faith that evening and ask a little more about Miss Allerdyce.

"Oh yes!" She said, "I have not seen her since the spring but we do have coffee sometimes and I certainly know that she would not mind if I were to speak to her and introduce you if you would like that? In fact, I could come tomorrow afternoon after school and we could call on her together and see if she could keep an eye open for Acajou as she lives near one of the houses you visit. I do have a hair appointment at half past five so I ought to leave when we have seen her but if you were to bring Toga, I could leave you to walk home if you don't mind. I would love to come with you and I know it would simplify matters if we go together the first time."

Leonie was so pleased; she knew Faith would do all she could to help anyone and she thanked her for being so understanding and offering to come so soon.

It was a quaint little cottage with an old-fashioned brass knocker on the door. Apprehensively, Leonie tapped but there was no response. After an appropriate pause, she knocked once more but with more vigour. There were footsteps on the stone flags within and then, the rattle of bolts being withdrawn and the upper half of the door, like that of a stable, was slowly opened. Miss Allerdyce had a deep, cultured voice and Leonie pictured a tall, thin woman with fading hair and eyes edged with crow's feet – a kindly soul.

"Good afternoon! It is so good to see you again, Faith,

The Feathered Refugees

and is this the friend you spoke to me about yesterday evening?" She spoke quietly, "Is there some way in which I could help you?"

Leonie explained her mission and she listened patiently. From within, there could be heard the sound of agitated clucking and scuffles and she excused herself and vanished for a moment. There was a clatter of tin plates and the texture of the sound was transformed into one of contentment: crooning and pecking beaks. She soon returned, apologising for the delay. "I was in the midst of preparing a meal for the chickens when you knocked," she said, "and the only way to quell the commotion was to serve it. Regrettably, some of the local residents have registered complaints to the council about the crowing of my cockerel and I am now forbidden to keep him or the hens in their run at the White Lodge. For the moment, my sitting-room is the only alternative."

Faith and Leonie commiserated with her and agreed that it was a sad state of affairs when the natural rural noises were to be abolished by decree and a young cockerel was no longer permitted to air his lungs and herald a new day. "Suffice it to say," she continued, "it grieves me greatly to have to muffle their existence, but we manage. Now, to your problem. I do still go regularly to the White Lodge for the grain with which I feed my refugees; it is stored with the straw in the rather dilapidated stable. I have seen the tray of food that you leave for your cat and I have been watching out for him since Mr Rider from Faversham Drive told me of his disappearance but I am afraid I have some bad news."

For a second or two Leonie began to hear a high-pitched whistling in her ears.

"It's a black cat," Miss Allerdyce continued, "who eats the food each morning. I have seen him quite often," she said, "and I am so sorry but it's not yours."

Leonie could breathe again. She had expected a far less pleasing disclosure and she knew full well that the food would tempt any creature that frequented the White Lodge haven.

Although Miss Allerdyce was presenting a brave face with the traditional English stiff upper lip, she sounded dejected as she depicted the clandestine way in which she was having to care for her beloved feathered charges and she forced a bright laugh when she said, "They all think I am just a crazy old woman and dismiss my behaviour as that of a crank but, cranky or not, I'll be only too pleased to put food down for you and to look out for your cat."

Saying how grateful she would be, Leonie handed her the tins she had brought with her and the stable door closed. Leonie sympathised with the "crankiness" of this compassionate woman, recognising a kindred spirit and was aware that she, too, could readily slip over the brink of custom when confronted with the maltreatment of animals.

The Feathered Refugees

In fact, Leonie recalled when she was about eleven years old at boarding school, while carrying a cheeping chicken in her pocket on the way down to breakfast, she had been caught and severely reprimanded by an astounded school matron for attempting to rear, in a cardigan nest in her bottom drawer, a tiny, yellow chick that she had purchased on an excursion to Watford market. It was only sixpence and the stall holder had been very generous and given her two for the price of one, probably because she was blind. On Saturday afternoons, the girls were allowed to go on a bus journey to one or two of the neighbouring towns, not more than six miles away, with a partner as long as one of them was partially sighted, and Watford seemed like an exciting adventure. The school she attended was especially for girls with limited or no sight and as only a few were totally blind, it made a good mix. She had believed that she was saving the chicken from a short life ending up too soon with a grizzly death in a cooking pot.

Faith warned Leonie as they parted that it was dusk and that she was almost invisible in her navy blue jacket and skirt. She suggested that she should not fold and put the white bag, in which she had brought the tins of cat food, into her pocket but carry it in order to make herself more conspicuous. With that and the white harness, she conceded that they could probably continue safely on the evening feeding round.

It was as she lay soaking up the warmth of the soothing, steamy atmosphere in the bath the same evening, that a fresh idea presented itself. Suchard and Paprika were grooming each other in preparation for sleep, contented with their environment. The slightest ripple of the water, however, soon aroused the cats and, as Leonie bestirred herself to more active ablutions, they began to play, each one showing their charming idiosyncrasies.

The bath was situated in a recess and Suchard liked to sit on the rim, preferably on the bath cleaning sponge, in a corner near the taps. The shower head above had a mesmerising tendency to drip and, now and then, with impeccably adjusted equilibrium, she extended a supinated paw to catch and drink a drop of water. Paprika would balance on the edge of the bath but, with less elegance, intermittently protesting at the sight of a naked body in the water. She used to be particularly upset as she witnessed a hair washing session and Leonie could only deduce that the transformation from slightly curled and moderately tidy hair to straight, wet straggles worried and confused her. Acajou, when at home, had liked to practise angling and, from his precarious perch on the rim of the bath, he used to pat any toe tips that protruded from the water. Sometimes, he forgot himself and grasped his prize more firmly with needle sharp claws as the game became too boisterous. When thirsty, he would walk to the end of

the bath to lean forward and tap the occupant gently on the shoulder. If the water was still free of soap, a cupped handful raised to his whiskers might tempt him to drink two or three mouthfuls before strolling back to the tap end to resume his fishing game.

When kittens, the washable nylon fur cat bed, whose ample dimensions permitted it simultaneously to accept three recumbent bodies, was placed beside the radiator. In the winter, a beach towel attached to the heated rail with pins and draped down and across the bed and tucked in underneath helped to protect them from the draught whistling under the door or through the windows. When the bathroom was chilly, the cats were restless and more inclined to be quarrelsome but the shade from the tent-like towelling structure seemed to lull them into a peaceful and more somnolent state. Inevitably, however, there were nights when it seemed impossible to curb their vivacity and Andrew and Leonie were brought rudely to their senses by a thunderous crash; the climax of a moonlit frisk seemed to have resulted in bottles of shampoo and a beaker of tooth brushes being knocked over and upsetting an overgrown orchid in a china pot.

There were also occasions when Paprika lifted the lid on Pandora's Box, so to speak, by managing to open the bathroom door herself and they were woken by a riotous frolicking on the stairs. There were two hooks on the bathroom door and if a dressing gown should be hanging on the one nearer to the door handle, having clambered up the rough towelling, she could hang on with three paws and reach out with the free one to press down on the handle, a horizontal bar design. As she swung on the dressing gown, her weight must have been sufficient to initiate movement at the hinge and the completion of the operation presented no difficulty for the eager claws waiting at floor level.

Seeing is Deceiving

As Leonie returned the soap and nail brush to the niche in the wall at the end of the bath and prepared to emerge from the water, Paprika's protestations provided her with a sudden inspiration. She leapt out of the bath, which made Paprika squawk even more volubly than usual her disapproval of the human form, and hurried to the bedroom to collect her pocket recorder. Pleased to be in the welcoming warm water once again, recorder in hand, Leonie waited. After all that commotion, the silence was profound. She agitated the water with her hand hoping to provoke a reaction. Then, assuming her plan had failed, she reached for the towel and was rewarded with a volley of rebukes, queries and complaints. Suchard mewed gently in agreement.

Armed with a splendid recording of feline voices, Toga and Leonie set forth the following morning, the 8th of November, on their routine dawn excursion with raised hopes. Passers-by must have been confused as, hand-in-pocket, repeatedly pressing the play button, it sounded as though Leonie was being pursued by protesting cats. Her strategy was, however, unproductive. She concluded that Acajou had become so timid that he dared no longer respond to the perfectly reproduced voices of his mother and his betrothed. There was, of course, a more realistic possibility: was he dead? Killed by a car?

Ignoring her waning optimism, Leonie dashed to the answerphone the moment she returned from her morning's work at the hospital. There was a message from her elder daughter to say that she would be coming home at the weekend to celebrate Leonie's birthday on the 12th.

Olivia was acutely fashion-conscious and she liked her mother to be smart so, as the salt was beginning to prevail over the pepper, Leonie decided to make an appointment with the hairdresser for a rejuvenating tint. The whole

The Feathered Refugees

operation could take up to two hours to complete so she decided to abbreviate the process as she was able, should necessity demand, to trim and curl her own hair. On Friday morning, with hair still wet and straight but with a natural brown restored, Leonie disguised herself with a scarf and ordered a taxi to take her home, dignity untarnished.

Andrew and Leonie had a happy weekend with Olivia who walked with her mother down to the Hoe and Sickle first thing on Sunday morning to see if they could find the cat described by the manager who had seen him on the lower steps of the fire escape. Having tossed some pieces of fish over the hedge, they stood perfectly still for a few moments – listening. There was a movement – and another, but Olivia could see nothing through the thick hedge. They then walked quietly to the gate and round to the fire escape on the other side of the hotel. Olivia gasped; a beautiful Siamese cat was just disappearing up to the top.

The door opened and the manager came out to greet them.

"You have seen the cat?" he said. Olivia explained that she had and as he had suggested, it did have a smart stripy tail. Sadly, he was not Acajou. Leonie thanked him for all his help and for telephoning her about seeing an unusual cat. They would just have to start again. Leonie was well aware that her veneer of merriment was paper-thin but she was determined to make the best of the day with Olivia. She was becoming increasingly conscious of the lowering clouds that threatened disappointment and she knew that the rest of the family were beginning to wish that she would accept the possible truth and relinquish the vain search. She knew she ought to acknowledge the fact that Acajou might have found another warm and comfortable home or been involved in an accident. However, she felt she owed it to him to continue the search as he was dependent upon her and, without her persistent effort, he would never make the journey home. The "hole in the doughnut" was expanding day by day.

On Monday morning, for the fourth consecutive week, Leonie contacted the *Chronicle* in order to insert a request in the Pet Column. Then, as she stood at the dressing table cogitating and applying a rosy hued illusion with a blusher brush in preparation for a hasty trip to the post office for some stamps, she was struck by what at that moment appeared to be a brilliant bolt out of the blue; another idea! The postmen – or were they by then called post persons? They were out at dawn each day and almost every house in Castleridge must be visited almost daily by one of them. She telephoned the post office straight away and a kindly sounding male voice agreed to put a notice up in the canteen.

The moment she replaced the handpiece, it vibrated wilfully so she picked it up again. It was a Radio Kent reporter responsible for the Pets' Corner wanting to know if the programme had produced any results.

"I would like to make one more really big effort on your behalf," she said, "and if you will give us permission, we will turn it into a news story featuring Toga and her hunt for her hitherto inseparable companion, the Burmese cat."

She then asked Leonie if she had any anecdotes to illustrate their friendship and, as Leonie responded, she could hear her scribbling and focusing her mind upon Acajou's now fading image; it helped Leonie to revive it into a three dimensional memory. They laughed together as Leonie described the way in which he defeated her efforts to restrict him to the house when she was leaving for work with Toga. Fitting snugly beneath the fairly long legged Labrador, protruding neither fore nor aft, he would sneak

The Feathered Refugees

out of the front door undetected by her scanning hand and follow them up the hill. As the distance between them increased, (there was no dallying for Toga on the way to the hospital in the mornings), Acajou would sometimes emit a soul-searing yowl; he was too afraid of the busy traffic to cross the road with them at the top of Pine Hill Avenue.

"Listeners love to hear stories about animals," the reporter assured her. "A story about a black Labrador guide dog searching high and low for her feline friend should have a tremendous appeal for the public and you might just be lucky."

"A story?" Leonie reflected, but that, she realised, was just part of the media jargon and she thanked her, pleased that she seemed interested and keen to help.

Leonie was so glad that she had chosen to work only in the mornings and she had always been able to rely on their loyal Miss Pepper who was willing to look after the children should they be unwell. She was also happy to take over in the afternoons if necessary. Occasionally, Leonie had to attend committee meetings in London and, four times a year, she travelled to a small town near Guildford where she was a governor in a school for teenaged youngsters with impaired vision.

When her children were still young, Leonie also took each child in turn as required by a model agency up to London and this provided a little money for them all to learn to ride and it was fun to look out for their advertisements on television. Olivia even found a picture of her blond haired brother once on a packet of Persil soap powder that she found in the cupboard under the kitchen sink. They rarely knew when the various photographic shoots they had done would be seen. In the holidays, Leonie sometimes took all three children to the Unicorn Theatre with her guide dog, Grace, at that time. On one occasion, the main character in the play, a dragon, had the same name and when summoned in a thunderous voice by the wicked king, the dog's reaction, to Leonie's chagrin, had caused quite a stir.

Her son used to love studying the underground maps on these adventures and, although only six or seven at this time, he relished telling his three-year-old and nine-year-old sisters exactly which platform they should be on and when Islington had been reached and how to find the Unicorn Theatre. On their train journey home, Leonie clearly remembered how Prudence, usually a fairly serious little girl, had discovered that, when imitating the persistent cough of another passenger in the carriage, she could make her brother and sister laugh at her surprising ability. Even Leonie was not used to this uncharacteristic and embarrassing behaviour and had to restrain her own mirth. Fortunately, however, the smoker himself seemed to find her amusing too.

Before catching the train to Craybridge for the sewing class that afternoon, Leonie delivered her notice to the post office plus a large tin of shortbread as a token of her gratitude for their co-operation and to encourage the post people to linger at the notice board and take due note.

Chapter 14

A Chill Wind

On Friday afternoon, 18th November, Celia Hammond phoned to enquire how the search was progressing for Acajou. "Well, let me see," she reflected aloud, "your cat has been away for almost a month now and the weather is becoming a little colder so we must speed things up if we can. The weeks do seem to add up in an alarming fashion," she murmured, "but we must not give up hope yet. I'll get Fiona who runs the Rescue Centre in Tunbridge Wells to contact the press and ask them to put the story in the local paper. If we write it from Toga's angle, the readers should be more interested and I'll see if we can arrange for some pictures to be taken."

Leonie thanked her profusely and promised to continue the search. Celia Hammond's positive attitude and enthusiasm were a tonic.

A couple of minutes later, Fiona rang and, shortly after that, a reporter from the *Castleridge Chronicle*. This was indeed action. The notice in the Pet Column had produced a few results, but a story and a photograph could revitalise the readers and the schoolchildren might start hunting afresh.

When Leonie took Toga out into the garden that night, she became aware of a marked change in the temperature. There was a sharp nip in the air. The long and unseasonably warm spell had come to an end and winter was beginning to take a hold. She shivered – and silently prayed once more. It always seemed to be easier to talk to God alone in the garden.

In church, she had the impression that He resided somewhere up at the front behind the pulpit and only on rare occasions did He enter her pew. That night, however, although He still seemed away above, somewhere in the purple velvet sky of a faintly recollected picture in a childhood storybook, in the cool, clear air, she felt that there was nothing to separate her from Him.

"Please," she begged, "take care of Acajou until we find him and could you show me where he is?"

If still leading a nomadic existence, Acajou would not be able to survive for long in frosty conditions nor withstand the rain and cold winds and consequent reduction in the food supply. He had never spent a night outside until this spell of absence.

On the following morning, Saturday 19th November, the skies were grey and overcast and fallen leaves scuttered before a bitter east wind. Christmas was now only five weeks away and as Andrew was going to be preoccupied with a project at work for the next two or three weekends, he suggested that they should go up to London to do some Christmas shopping. He had been incredibly patient and understanding and so generous with his time over the last month helping her to look for Acajou when many other things were requiring his attention, that Leonie agreed to go. She could shop alone with Toga locally for selected presents but, with Andrew, they could look for new ideas in the big London stores. She had already planned Andrew's Christmas surprise, having been able to buy a voucher for his first experience of carriage driving. He had been uncertain about horses when young but, having held her horse's head at various events until it was her turn

A Chill Wind

to compete, he had become accustomed to them and had begun to appreciate their different personalities. In fact, he showed a natural aptitude for controlling the horse or horses with skilful hands on the long reins and gently spoken commands and it became a regular Saturday morning activity and a hobby they could both share.

There had been no phone calls about sightings of Acajou for a few days now and Leonie knew that Andrew had accepted the fact that they would probably never see him again.

They shopped briefly for essentials in the local supermarket and decided to go by train to London after an early lunch.

"Just going to look at the rugby on television for ten minutes." Andrew called from the sitting room as Leonie went upstairs to change. A short rest would help him to recharge his batteries and Leonie was only too pleased to procrastinate as long as possible. With a little luck, she thought, he might just nod off for a moment or two and she would be within reach of the telephone for a few extra minutes.

It was a quarter to two before Leonie heard Andrew moving again downstairs.

"Ok, dear, nearly ready?" he called.

Having already changed her shoes she put on her coat and, with a leaden heart, switched the answerphone to recording mode. Toga came quickly when she heard the lead being lifted from its hook.

"Keys, money, cheque book?" Andrew patted his various pockets and was just closing the front door when the telephone rang. Somewhat irritably, he strode in to answer it. The next train was due to leave at seventeen minutes past two and it was a thirteen minute walk to the station at a good speed.

"No, we haven't," Leonie heard him say rather brusquely, she thought, and then his tone changed. "Thank you so much! Where are you? Yes, we'll come straight away. Goodbye. It's Acajou!" He said. "At least, it was a very good description; that was Rosemary Martin, number four, St. Mary's Drive. If I dash up in the car, you could come on with Toga when you have picked up some titbits for Acajou and if you bring your car key, you will know where I am." His own car keys were already in his hand and he was gone. Leonie was suddenly overwhelmed with an injection of fresh energy and an all-pervading sense of elation.

Imbued with the contagion of excitement, Toga yawned loudly and wriggled uncontrollably when Leonie put on her harness. As the shops were crowded at that time of year, they had originally decided to use a lead in London as Leonie would have held Andrew's hand in the crowds and it would not have been possible for Toga to guide under those circumstances. Her pocket filled, she banged the door behind her and they dashed up Pine Hill Avenue. Leonie listened carefully as they crossed the two roads at the top which met in a forked junction, then turned into St Mary's Drive. She did not know where exactly number four was situated but her car key would help. Having walked a short distance down the Drive, she began pressing the button on the key waiting to hear a click of unlocking doors. Ah, there it was. She walked towards the sound while continuing to lock and unlock until she almost reached the car when Toga took over and decided they needed to find the door and wait for the driver. Leonie stood still and listened. Toga stood still too. It might not have been possible to park outside number four so they walked up and down the road just listening but there was no sound. Andrew was not there. As the gardens of these houses adjoined the land belonging to the derelict nursery, Leonie

A Chill Wind

decided to go back to the top of the Drive and turn left to see if the nursery gates were open. They were. Having turned in through the entrance, they had only walked a few steps when there was a crunching sound beneath her feet. Probably broken glass – she stopped instantly lest Toga's paws should be lacerated. Bending down swiftly, she wrapped her arms around Toga's chest and hind legs to carry her struggling back out on to the pavement where she shook herself vigorously and sat as commanded so that Leonie could inspect her paws, gently feeling each pad with her finger-tips. She could find no splinters of glass and, as Toga seemed unperturbed, she presumed that all was well. Having recovered their equanimity, she called Acajou hoping that her voice would carry into the hinterland of Crester's Nursery. Infinitely slowly, the seconds ticked by – no response.

"Ah, there you are." It was Andrew. "I have just been around the nursery. Don't go in; a bull dozer has started to knock down all the greenhouses and there's a fearful mess everywhere. I'm afraid there's no sign of Acajou."

"What exactly did Rosemary Martin say to you?" Leonie asked.

"She said she had just returned from the shops and the children had told her about a strange cat they had seen at the far end of the garden approximately half an hour earlier."

Half an hour, two hours ago, three days, it was always the same but Leonie was not too downhearted this time and she had no intention of giving up at this stage.

"Did you knock on Rosemary's door?" she persisted. He had not. She smiled inwardly. Men! "Let's go then," she proposed cheerily, "to see if she can give us any more clues."

Of course, Mrs Martin was expecting them and she took

them through to the sitting room with French windows that opened out on to the garden and quietly, they walked down to the far end. She told them then just what had happened.

"Simpkin, my tabby kitten," she said, "was sitting on the window sill after lunch surveying the chilly garden from his warm vantage point, I assume, and apparently he started to make some odd staccato sounds. Rosanne, my nine-year-old, ran to the window to see what was attracting his attention and she saw this cat, a complete stranger, so she called Christopher, my son, to see if he recognised it. It's a gloomy old day though, isn't it, and I think the cat looked almost black. Christopher, however, realised immediately that it was a Burmese because there are two further down the road and then he remembered the note on the lamp post and also the one that had come through the door two or three weeks ago. Rosanne recalled that a green collar had been mentioned so she ran down the garden to look. He was wearing a green collar but her footsteps had frightened him and he slipped away through a hole in the fence which, as you can see, is almost six feet high and neither of the children could see over the top. When I came back from the shops, Rosanne told me all this and I rummaged through the pile of letters and odd pieces of paper on the dresser – and there it was, your note, so I phoned you straight away. I do so hope it was your cat and that we'll see him again."

By this time, they were standing fairly near the shed. Toga whimpered. Softly, Leonie called. Andrew was in the shed looking under and behind all the clutter that tends to accumulate in garden sheds, but it was a grey afternoon and the light was poor and he could not see Acajou. Then, there was a low, mournful wail followed by a fluttering of wings and the repeated cries of a distressed ringdove as it

A Chill Wind

rose up from behind the fence. There was another sound... "Was that a cat?" Leonie wondered aloud. Rosemary agreed it could have been but Andrew dismissed the idea, certain that it was a disturbed and agitated bird – but there it was again; a definite "meow" and it was in a minor key! Toga whined again and pulled so hard on the lead that Leonie had to pick up the harness handle to restrain her. She was desperately anxious that Toga should not frighten Acajou with her effusive welcome. Andrew called once more and again, he was answered – and again. Toga began to tremble and to wag her tail so violently that her whole body moved in sympathy. Her whining then reached an ear-splitting crescendo and Leonie could hardly control her in her excitement. Acajou had not seen her for a whole month and he might conceivably have developed a fear of dogs. Leonie stroked Toga under the chin and attempted to soothe her with whispered words of reassurance. Her exuberance must not deter him.

"It's Acajou, I can see him – come on then, this way – come on." Andrew was speaking in a gentle, coaxing manner. Leonie held her breath and Rosemary whispered in her ear, "I can see him now and he's walking very slowly and seems to be limping."

"There, it's alright now," she heard Andrew say as he bent down to pick him up. "And you are still wearing that green collar with the disc and the bell too but that looks a bit rusty." He crooned to Acajou with quiet words of comfort. You are like an old piece of string," he murmured, "and what a thin, scraggy boy you are – but you will be alright now." And he walked over to Leonie with Acajou in his arms.

Remembering the stern Scottish tones of Toga's ex-Army officer guide dog trainer, Leonie commanded her firmly to sit, down and stay! It worked like a charm and

Seeing is Deceiving

she flattened herself on the ground, tail still wagging. With her free hand, she touched Acajou and, caressing him gently, she kissed him between the ears. Somewhat embarrassed, she tried to blink away tears and silently, she had a quick word with God.

"Poor old thing," Andrew continued, "you are just a bag of bones. In fact, I have never seen anything more like a Lowry match stick cat – and no one read the phone number on your disc."

The fur around Acajou's eyes was encrusted and there were scabs by his nose, under his chin and on the back of his head, partially healed wounds on his legs and bald patches on his flank.

"Oh Acajou, what have you been up to?" But he answered only with a deep throated purr; a rumble of appreciation.

Rosemary was almost as thrilled as Leonie.

"I lost a Siamese cat once," she told them, "so I know how you both feel – but we never did find him and I still wonder what became of him. Perhaps Acajou has been hiding in one of those greenhouses that they began to knock down in the nursery yesterday? He wasn't in the shed, I know, because the children looked in there when we received your note. Besides, there's a hole in the back wall and it's a regular thoroughfare for all the local cats who come through that loose panel on the fence and would have flushed him out on their way to the overgrown garden behind the Methodist church."

Acajou was beginning to struggle a little and Rosemary went back to the house to find her wicker cat basket. It was beginning to rain with a few flecks of snow blowing in the wind.

"We must get you home old thing." Andrew said, his finger hooked firmly through the green collar as he continued to stroke and to calm him. Rosanne and Christopher were

A Chill Wind

with Rosemary when she returned with the cat basket but they were shy and said little. They had been watching through the window. Acajou did not enjoy being put into the cat basket which resembled a cage and he raised loud objections all the way to the car. His feeble raging soon subsided, and Toga, who was sitting beside him, tried to thrust her wet nose between the narrow bars of the cage door. She snuffled and sniffed at him eventually managing to reach one of his ears with her extended tongue. Gradually, he relaxed and began to purr.

Temporarily, they shut Suchard and Paprika in the sitting-room in order to ensure a controlled reintroduction and Leonie took Acajou out of the carrier to settle him on the woolly rug on top of the warm kitchen boiler. He crawled into the darkest corner behind the broad flu pipe purring continuously, but it was a harsh and rasping sound. His throat was dry and probably sore and he kept opening and closing his mouth as though trying to yawn. He did not seem to see the saucer of creamy milk that Leonie had put in front of him.

She telephoned the vet and was informed that the on-call vet for the afternoon lived in Oxstead, fifteen or so miles away from Castleridge. However, the Oxstead vet advised them to keep Acajou at home rather than submit him to a long car journey and possibly more unpleasant experiences. He said that the only treatment he could recommend was to keep him warm and give him water to drink from a tea spoon, as frequently as possible, until he became less dehydrated. Acajou would not put out his tongue to lap the water in the spoon so Andrew filled an eye drop dispenser and with this he was able regularly to moisten his mouth.

While Leonie continued to try and calm him and settle him down to sleep, Andrew took the cat basket and an envelope containing their promised reward to Rosanne and Christopher.

There was a frenzied scratching at the kitchen door and, as Paprika was wont to damage the carpet when on the wrong side of a door, Leonie left the kitchen for a moment to go and talk to the girls who were waiting in the hall. She picked them both up and carried them through to the sitting-room where she could reassure them and give them some individual attention. Suddenly, there was a nasty thud and she dashed back to the kitchen where, walking cautiously, she found Acajou lying on the floor and realised how foolish she had been to leave him up on top of the boiler so soon. He stirred when she touched him and, slowly, he stood up and walked towards the door but he was limping and clearly in pain.

"No more boiler tops for you, my boy!"

She found a cardboard box and put in it a warm hot water bottle wrapped with one of Toga's recently laundered blankets. He seemed to be quite content to curl up on the bottle and she placed the box on the floor in the corner near Toga's basket. Gently, she moved each one of his limbs in turn, examining the joints in an endeavour to discover the extent of the damage. The outside toe on the right hind paw was completely flaccid and probably fractured. The whole leg seemed to be held in rotation and the hip, possibly dislocated, protruded in an abnormal manner. As Leonie tested each movement, prepared to stop should there be the slightest wince, Acajou lay inert. There was gross effusion around the right wrist and just above his elbow on the same limb, there was a hard lump; perhaps a small piece of bone still attached to the muscle avulsed at its insertion. This limb too lay in an abnormal posture and Leonie had heard a sickening crack in the region of the shoulder at every step. His coat was

A Chill Wind

dull, his eyes sunken and he was pathetically emaciated; he was indeed a very sick cat!

A car door slammed. Andrew had returned and together, they pored over the invalid more closely to study his injuries. Fur had begun to grow over partially healed wounds on his legs which led them to believe that they had occurred several days ago and almost certainly, simultaneously. The fact that most of the injuries seemed to be on one side and apparently of an equivalent duration, reinforced their conviction that Acajou had been hit by a car.

"No wonder the poor chap is dehydrated," Andrew commented; "with all these injuries, he would not have been able to walk far enough to reach food and water, let alone catch anything on the hoof. His ear has been bitten too. I suspect this happened before a car accident when tussling with or for a potential breakfast."

Two hours and half a dozen eyedropper loads later, Acajou was able to take his first independent lap of water and, soon after this, to swallow a mouthful of fish. Seemingly satisfied, he then elongated himself on the blanket in a characteristically feline stretch and the deep throated purr died away. He lay perfectly still. With trembling fingers, Leonie touched his ribs and waited. From the moment they had found him, Leonie had been cognisant of the fact that he might not survive as he was in such a poor state. He had at least experienced comforting warmth and love once again and he must have known he had not been forsaken. Kneeling beside him, she leaned forward to put her face near his in order to see if she could feel his breath on her cheek.

For what seemed an eternity, there was absolute silence. As she touched him again, his whiskers twitched and he sighed. She stroked him gently. His respiration was shallow but regular now and she pulled a piece of the blanket over him and left him to sleep.

    Without delay, she phoned Olivia, Thomas and Prudence, but she had a long wait to pass the good news on to her elder daughter as she could not respond to the hospital bleep for a few minutes. Leonie rarely phoned as she never knew exactly when Olivia would be on duty but she could keep the wonderful news to herself no longer. Olivia was stunned – hour after hour and day after day, she had waited for this moment, Olivia said, imagining herself being called away from a ward round or meeting but she had begun to give up hope. She knew that her mother would not be happy until the search had been concluded; the uncertainty was intolerable.

    "I'll come home," she began but the bleep abruptly ended her conversation and she promised to call later.

    Next, she phoned her son, Thomas, and he, too, was amazed and delighted. He wanted to hear every detail of the recovery and was distressed to learn of Acajou's multiple injuries. He was, however, keen to tell his mother all his news too. He was eager to tell her to stop buying bottled still water as one of their experiments this week had shown that there were more bacteria than in an equivalent bottle of pond water. Sparkling water was, he said, a little better probably as the carbonic acid might kill some of the bugs. He also told her about the weekend which he had spent with a friend in his highland castle where he had been required to kill and pluck his own dinner, to sleep in a four poster bed and had been brought a jug of cold water for the marble topped wash stand for his morning ablutions.

    "There was a priest hole in my bedroom," he added, "and arrows in the passages to guide me to breakfast in the dining room. I had no idea Hamish was a real live Scottish laird!" and he laughed. They had spent a whole

A Chill Wind

year together at Edinburgh University and on the same course.

Their younger daughter, Prudence, was harder to contact, especially on a Saturday afternoon when she could be out rowing or rehearsing with her oboe in the university orchestra. Leonie decided they would wait until Prudence phoned later in the evening to tell her parents more about her exciting new life and to catch up with the family news. Instead, Leonie rang both Faith and Madeleine, her school teacher friends. Faith had helped her so much during the half term break, walking with her in unfamiliar territory and later, taking her to find Miss Allerdyce, the lady who rescued traumatised chickens.

As it was only five o'clock and Acajou was sleeping peacefully, Andrew suggested that they should nip up to the Art Shop to buy some Christmas cards so that he could occupy himself profitably during the evening; this was a task that usually fell to Andrew but one he quite willingly undertook. For Leonie it was a more laborious activity. She could have addressed the envelopes with her word processor and she could guess where to inscribe their good wishes followed by her signature but it took her a long time. Also, Andrew's address book contained all the addresses of his colleagues to whom he liked to send a card with an added message.

The temperature outside was dropping rapidly and the rain had turned to sleet. The forecast on the six o'clock news promised the first snow fall of the winter. Acajou had been found with only moments to spare: had they closed the front door and left for London, it would have been too late.

Faith, who had slipped up to the High Street to make some last minute purchases, caught sight of Andrew and Leonie through a shop window whilst choosing their cards

Seeing is Deceiving

and she popped in to share her pleasure at their good news. She seemed to be genuinely delighted that the story had a happy ending, confiding that she had hardly dared hope for this. As a teenager, she had lost her beloved spaniel, Moss, in the Otford Hills and in spite of endless searching and patient waiting, he had never come home.

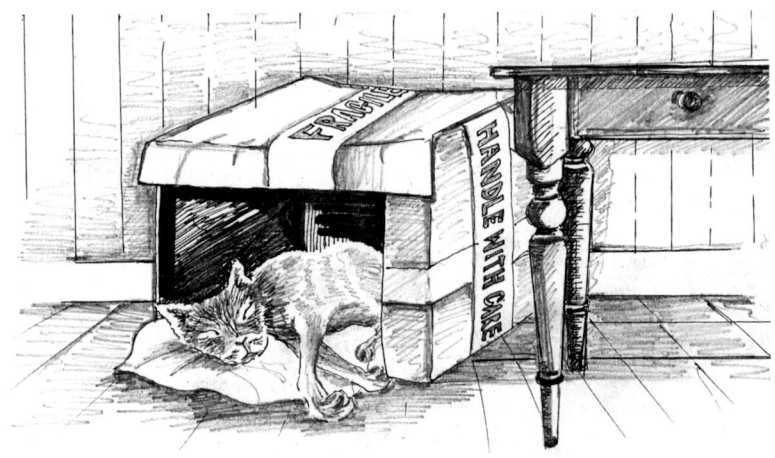

Soon after their return, Madeleine arrived to see the treasured invalid herself and to add her felicitations. She was, however, distressed when she saw his poor condition and revealed at a later date that, having seen his wasted body and twisted limbs with unhealed wounds, she had doubted that he would live through the night.

Acajou was unable to climb out of his box without assistance and Leonie marvelled at the fact that he had been able to walk into Rosanne and Christopher's garden and come to them when they had called. When and where, she wondered, had he had his accident with the car? From observation of the skin growth on the wounds, Andrew surmised that it might had been about two weeks ago, November 5th, Guy Fawkes' night? That was a possibility.

A Chill Wind

Had he dashed across a road, heedless of the traffic, terrified by exploding fireworks? Could it be that the racket created by the bulldozers, the splintering wood and shattering glass had woken him from his twilight sleep in some dark corner as the nursery as buildings were razed to the ground? Was the spark of fear fanned by the uproar around him into a flame of desire to survive? His fragile spirit could have been extinguished and his body crushed in the mayhem.

Leonie carried the cardboard box plus its occupant from the kitchen into the sitting room where she put it down on the floor near the radiator. Suchard eyed him suspiciously from a healthy distance, not attempting to move from her chosen spot on the piano stool. Cautiously, Paprika approached to within three feet and then, her tail fully fluffed, emitted a strange, low growl. Eventually, Suchard could contain her curiosity no longer. She jumped down from the piano stool and slowly walked towards Acajou while he lay still on his blanket, completely unmoved by the presence of his audience. To reassure her, Leonie picked Suchard up but she stiffened in her arms and spat in the direction of the cardboard box. Poor old Acajou! They did not recognise him and he probably smelt rather unusual.

With a disinfected cloth that had been dipped into a bowl of warm water and thoroughly squeezed, Leonie washed his face and sponged his coat for he was too weak to wash himself and she realised that it would be a while until he could participate in the mutual grooming that binds a feline family. Both the girls left the room and went upstairs to spend the evening curled up together on Prudence's bed. Toga was far more amenable; she lay on the bean bag beside Acajou, intermittently wagging her tail, now and then resting her chin on the edge of the box to sniff him or to proffer the odd clumsy lick.

Seeing is Deceiving

A thin layer of snow covered the ground and crunched beneath Leonie's feet as she took Toga out into the garden to relieve herself before going to bed. With Acajou home once again tucked up in the cardboard box on a refilled hot water bottle, instead of dreading the falling temperature, she could enjoy the exhilaration that comes with the first cold, crisp night of winter when the landscape is blanketed with snow and all the man-made blemishes are temporarily obliterated; the perfect setting for her expression of gratitude.

It was plain that the girls would not welcome Acajou in the bathroom that night nor did Leonie dare to leave him out of earshot, so she and Andrew decided that he should sleep in their bedroom. This, Leonie felt, was a real achievement for, until about ten years ago, Andrew was certain that he was not keen on cats. Then, attending a sports event at Thomas's prep school, he had been fascinated and intrigued by two Burmese kittens who performed the most amazing gymnastic feats with elegance and precision that would have befitted circus-trained acrobats. Having discovered this chink in his armour, the children had soon lured him to a stud farm which happened also to have a litter of Burmese kittens. The deed was done and they left with a milk chocolate coloured kitten who had a kink at the tip of her tail and the price had been reduced because this prevented her from becoming a show cat. Suchard had entered their lives! Having twisted Andrew around her little claw, she was followed one year and a day later by her son, Acajou, and his four sisters. A handsome brown Burmese male, a National Champion, had been selected for mating with her. Leonie remembered only too vividly the journey on a train with Suchard, the reluctant bride, cringing unhappily in the corner of the cat basket. Negotiating Chislehurst station had been the trickiest part of the journey, finding the stairs and keeping up with the footsteps of the other disembarking passengers in order to reach the exit with Toga in one hand and Suchard in the other. She was well acquainted with the geography of Castleridge station so that had not presented a problem.

It was horrid leaving Suchard, timid and bewildered, with the breeder but she had been told, in a distinctly no-nonsense manner, that the betrothal and honeymoon period would have to last a minimum of three days and, in any case, Leonie was assured, there was infra-red heating beneath the bed and all mod cons in the cage which took pride of place in the Chislehurst garden. Mrs P. Heatherington-Browne had been somewhat surprised to find Toga had been virtually responsible for bringing them both all the way from Castleridge to her house. She had wondered why Leonie had required so much detail when asking for directions.

Paprika, who was a month younger than Acajou, had joined the household when she was twelve weeks old. Having formed a secret liaison with Acajou, she surprised Andrew and Leonie by producing three beautiful kittens when she was only seven months old. These were skilfully delivered by Suchard who nipped the umbilical cords and washed each kitten as it arrived on the cats' cushion behind the armchair near the piano in the sitting room. Acajou was far less helpful and just looked on in amazement as though he had had nothing to do with the whole affair. He was even caught having a crafty sip of milk from time to time when the intended beneficiaries were not actively engaged in procuring a meal.

In their bedroom, there was a winged back chair that Leonie had been taking to upholstery classes. It had been in a three-quarters finished state since the course ended in the summer and, although the chair was entirely covered by a figured gold material, the panel at the back was only secured by pins, as Leonie was still working on it when the spirit moved her. Leonie draped an old sheet over it, protected the cushion with a black dustbin bag and moved it so that the front of the seat and the arms were up against the side of the bed. Refilling the hot water bottle once more, she placed the cardboard box on its side on the cushion so that by merely putting one hand out from beneath the duvet, she would be able to check him during the night. If he were to move, she would know immediately as he could only come towards her. Newspaper was laid out on the carpet and a litter brought in and put under the dressing table. She marvelled at Andrew's changed attitude! A saucer of water and a little food were placed on the paper. At first, Acajou settled down most obligingly but, just after midnight, a dismal and penetrating howl pierced her dreams. She slid her hand over the edge of the mattress and straight on to the chair to stroke and to pacify him but he was restless. Stepping out of bed and being careful not to put her toes in the cold water, Leonie took Acajou from the box and put him down beside the food. He licked the water but declined the food and the litter. He had not yet used the litter since his return and she was anxious to know that his kidneys were still functioning. When back in the box, he settled down to sleep once more but an hour or so later, the whole performance was repeated.

 Just after three o'clock, the corner of the duvet was gently pulled from her face and a paw extended to touch Leonie's cheek. With a little assistance, Acajou crawled under the duvet to curl up on her chest enfolded in her arms. This was the moment Leonie had dreamed of for the last four weeks and she relished every second. Never would Acajou have a narrower squeak; a whisker away from annihilation! When he was picked up by Andrew

A Chill Wind

at the end of Rosemary's garden, she had told them that they usually visited her mother on a Saturday. It was so fortunate that they were home and that Christopher and Rosanne had been watching Simpkin as he looked intently down the garden. It was then that Acajou had been seen and his rescue was miraculous!

Acajou was gradually regaining a little strength and, having licked the fragment of fish and lapped the water once more, he resisted the cardboard box and insisted on returning to the bed where he slowly settled down, easing his injured leg into a comfortable position beside the pillow with his head resting on it and a paw on Leonie's neck. He had always seemed to draw pleasure, or possibly a feeling of companionship, from the sensation of warm skin on his cool paw. There he slept without stirring until morning when the first light made Andrew visible. He decided to totter across the top of the pillow and woke Andrew with a loving head butt before quietly settling down beside him to sleep again until the alarm clock woke them at seven. He was as happy to be home again as Andrew and Leonie were to have found him.

During the next few days, Acajou wailed whenever he discovered he was alone for a few minutes but the touch of a human hand or a communication from Toga soon calmed him. Paprika and Suchard kept their distance for several days whereas normally all three cats used to enjoy games together but they would not even share the cat cushion. Toga, however, seemed to understand that he was unwell and she was uncharacteristically gentle with him.

Chapter 15

Idiosyncrasies

The games begun when the cats were apparently in a sleeping heap were many and varied. A provocative prod of a paw might be followed by a nip of a twitching tail and a mild struggle would result in a leap to freedom of one of the cats before the chance of being unceremoniously pushed. These sessions could soon become wilder and include the hurling of verbal insults while Leonie was trying to talk on the telephone. They would vie for her attention. Acajou used to start the trouble by taking up his position on the narrow shelf beneath the telephone looking down at the others while making challenging gestures. Should the game of poking and counter thrust become too hectic, he could scramble up on to the top of the table and thence up on to Leonie's shoulder where, with a pendulous movement of the tail and a teasing forelimb of seemingly limitless length, he would initiate another stage in the mock battle. A paw in mid-flight could cause considerable confusion, bringing a conversation to an abrupt end should it contact one of the telephone keys. The girls demonstrated their desire to be noticed in other ways. When the phone upstairs on the dressing table was being used, Paprika would pick up and play with Leonie's lipstick or mascara. If nothing sufficiently interesting was available, she was able to raise the roof of the small Swiss chalet, bought on Leonie's first school trip abroad, in which loose beads and

Idiosyncracies

a couple of buttons, a curtain hook, a broken watch strap and a half empty cotton reel were stored. Any one of these items could give pleasure but the most popular was a tail end of thread which she could take deftly between her teeth and pull until the reel stopped spinning.

Suchard was less bold when trying to communicate with Leonie but her technique was no less effective. She was the first kitten to arrive and it took Leonie a little while to learn to avoid treading on her. She wore soft shoes when in the house so that if a small paw or tail tip should be crushed, the damage would be minimal. As a small kitten, however, Suchard soon learned that her briefest mew would instantly arrest Leonie's progress. She realised that it was risky weaving around her ankles for more than a moment or two, even though she wished to be stroked or picked up, so, in order to alert Leonie to the fact that she wanted to be fed or caressed, she mewed clearly and repeatedly after which she rubbed herself and her collar with its bell against the nearest door post and waited. She seemed to know that the sound would guide Leonie to her. This seemed to be a fanciful notion but Andrew watched her and said that it appeared to be remarkable but true. Another of her quaint idiosyncrasies

was her desire to observe life from the highest point and indoors, this frequently involved balancing on the top of an open door. Leonie was always careful when closing a door as this could have caused a catastrophe. When working at the kitchen table, she often heard the clink of china and she knew that the cupboard door had been opened. As Suchard made her upward progress passing the cups and plates, the larger dishes and then the jams and marmalade, she recognised the different sounds and knew Suchard was making her way up to the dusty top of the cupboard to purr in ecstasy prowling amongst the emergency candles, the Braille recipe and physiotherapy books, the spare box of breakfast cereal and the camping kettle. By standing with one foot on the table and the other on the dresser, Leonie could usually retrieve her before too much damage was done. The spare light bulbs on top of the books caused her the most concern. Occasionally, the odd quiescent amaryllis lily or dislodged candle had surprised an unwitting visitor as it tumbled seven or eight feet down on to the tiled kitchen floor.

Throughout Sunday, Andrew and Leonie continued the hourly drips of water and were delighted when the patient used the litter tray for the first time that evening. All those whose help had been enlisted during the search for Acajou had asked Leonie to let them know if, by any chance, he was found. As soon as she returned from the hospital at lunch time on Monday having now discovered that the mysterious caller had been sitting in the waiting room while she had been discussing cat rescue telephone numbers with the receptionist, Leonie decided to make some phone calls. She contacted Celia Hammond first. There were so many people and organisations to whom she needed to show her gratitude. (RSPCA, The Register of Burmese Cats in Gloucester, Cats Any Time in Orpington and the woman from the Burmese Cat Club in London.)

The reporter from the local paper, in which Celia Hammond had hoped to have a story about Acajou printed, phoned for more details and seemed to be disappointed when Leonie told him the hunt was over, the treasure found and it was no longer necessary to publish the article. Throughout the day, several others telephoned to say that they had heard the joyous news and how pleased they were for her. She decided to write a special note to Miss Allerdyce, the chicken lady.

Lillian, her next door neighbour, who herself owned two fine Siamese cats, called to see Acajou at lunch time. She was very sad to see what a poor state he was in and asked if he had been seen by a vet. Leonie told her that they had been advised to look after him quietly at home but kindly, Lillian offered to take her to the local surgery in the car that evening as she thought that it would probably set their minds at rest. She accepted the offer and agreed that she would be happier if he were to be thoroughly examined as she was keen to know what more she could do to hasten his recovery. Lillian came for Leonie at a quarter past five and they tucked Acajou with a warm bottle and a blanket into the box. He didn't have the strength to struggle so it was an easy journey. The vet inspected him carefully moving each limb gently and reached the conclusion that he was not well enough to be subjected to the procedures involved in an X-ray. He would probably have to be anaesthetised and he was too weak and malnourished for this risk to be taken. He removed the incrustations from around his eyes. He cleaned the wounds and cut away the matted fur before giving him two injections: an anabolic steroid more rapidly to promote an increase in body weight and the other, a slow acting antibiotic. He clipped his jagged and broken claws and reiterated that tender loving care was the only other medicine that she could safely offer him and, he laughed, the odd prayer might help. He could make no promises about Acajou's prognosis but he did say that if he should still be alive and somewhat fitter in three or four weeks' time, he would like to see him again and check on the various sites of skeletal damage.

"Weakness and pain," he said, "will prevent too much movement and that might give his fractures a chance to heal without further treatment. The antibiotic, of course, will help to control infection in his wounds."

Leonie took Acajou home feeling relieved that he had been professionally assessed and to know that she was doing all that she possibly could do for him. Restored once more to his box, Acajou seemed quite contented although he did not purr, nor had he done so since Saturday afternoon when he had probably exhausted himself by a prolonged and a fortissimo use of that mysterious purring mechanism.

When Leonie returned from work on Tuesday afternoon, Miss Pepper, their long time and faithful house cleaner had spent the morning looking after him. Leonie tried to encourage him to eat but he declined everything she proffered. He mewed frequently which Leonie felt was possibly stimulated by hunger. She tried freshly cooked fish, she tried meat, she dipped his paw in some cream and then gave up but, still stroking him, she settled him over her shoulder while preparing a little lunch for herself. When she opened the bread bin to take out the wholemeal loaf in order to make a tomato sandwich, he made a sudden darting movement towards her hand. He bit the crust voraciously and started to eat. Never before had he bothered with this type of food! Perhaps stale crusts put out for the birds had been his staple diet during his leave of absence? He had apparently tried to hunt as there was a bite on one ear, another on his neck and one on his right front paw. He relished this bread and its recognition had been instant. Thereafter, she added small broken pieces of bread to his meals and it worked like magic! The smell of it seemed to rekindle his appetite and he appeared to remember that with this, his hunger could be assuaged.

The repair of cat relationships was more difficult to achieve and it was not until the 28th of November, nine days after coming home, that Paprika was prepared to share a chair with him. Two days later, her example was followed by Suchard. Mutual grooming sessions recommenced and it was marvellous to see once again the three cats entwined in harmony.

Acajou's progress was slow but fairly sure. The gloss returned to his coat, bald areas began to sprout new fur and, although he continued to walk with a pronounced limp, he began to move around the house with greater ease. On the 2nd of December, he started to purr again and on the following Thursday evening, he strolled into the bathroom to eat his supper and then settled down in the communal bed as though he had never been away. Cautiously, the girls joined him, Paprika nestling around the curve of his bony spine and Suchard intermingling chin and paws so that they fitted together like pieces of a jigsaw puzzle.

The picture was complete; Acajou had once more resumed his rightful place in the feline family.

About the Author

Anne Whittenbury lost her sight at the age of six in an accidental explosion at home. Educated at Chorleywood College for Blind and Partially Sighted Girls and having been to a film of a hospital drama in the school holidays, she chose to train as a physiotherapist in preference to studying law. She became the first blind physiotherapist at Guy's Hospital, London, where she met her future husband. She was awarded a scholarship in the United States to demonstrate that physiotherapy could be a profession for blind people and to participate in advanced methods of rehabilitation in California. Her appetite for life has been demonstrated by the love of challenges with sporting activities: horse riding, dancing, swimming and both water and cross-country skiing. Through the years, her five guide dogs have been an invaluable assistance to her professional work and in raising a family of three children. She has had many different hobbies including, most recently, designing and modelling ceramic sundials.